MARKS OF METHODISM

Grant,

History as theology and theology as history.

Russ

VOLUME 5

UNITED
METHODISM AND
AMERICAN
CULTURE

MARKS OF METHODISM

THEOLOGY IN ECCLESIAL PRACTICE

Russell E. **Richey**

with

Dennis M. **Campbell**

and

William B. **Lawrence**

Abingdon Press

Nashville

UNITED METHODISM AND AMERICAN CULTURE, VOLUME 5
MARKS OF METHODISM: THEOLOGY IN ECCLESIAL PRACTICE

Copyright © 2005 by Abingdon Press

This book is printed on acid-free paper.

Library of Congress Cataloging-in-Publication Data

Richey, Russell E.
   Marks of Methodism : theology in ecclesial practice / Russell E. Richey, with Dennis M. Campbell and William B. Lawrence.
      p. cm. — (United Methodism and American culture ; v. 5)
   ISBN 0-687-32939-6 (pbk. : alk. paper)
   1. Methodist Church. 2. Wesley, John 1703-1791. I. Campbell, Dennis M., 1945- II. Lawrence, William B. (William Benjamin), 1946- III. Title. IV. Series.

   BX8331.3.R53 2005
   287—dc22

                                                                                    2004026776

05 06 07 08 09 10 11 12 13 14—10 9 8 7 6 5 4 3 2 1
MANUFACTURED IN THE UNITED STATES OF AMERICA

*To My
Mother,*

Erika Richey,

*Christian
Practitioner*

Contents

Methodist Practices

The Wesleys, John and Charles, and the peoples called Methodist, we believe, have imbedded their deepest convictions, their most cherished values, their defining beliefs, and their fondest hopes in practices. On that premise, we argue here that one way to do theology in the Wesleyan spirit is to read practices theologically.[1]

Those with a passing familiarity with the movement know or know about Methodist practices—hymns, love feasts, conferences, class meetings, journal-keeping, testimony, discipline, itinerancy, and so forth. Many students of Methodism will also know that its founders wrote extensively in virtually every religious mode save one, systematic theology. Systematics was not the forte of either John or Charles Wesley.

Nor has systematic theology been one of Methodism's strengths. Recognizing that, Methodist interpreters have coped intellectually in several ways. Some apologists for Wesleyanism, from very early days to the present, have endeavored to compensate for the failure and to render a credible Wesleyan systematic. Others have conceded that John Wesley and Methodists generally have functioned best as evangelical theologians. These interpreters, therefore, have concerned themselves with evangelical doctrines and have focused on soteriology and saving work. Still others have not worried so much over the matter of systematics and have proceeded to invest themselves intellectually in other theological endeavors—philosophy of religion, ethics, and social ethics, biblical studies, historical theology, and of course, various practical theologies. In various ways, then, Methodists have countered the accusation made by others, especially by those in the Reformed tradition, that we are theologically wanting.

Here we pursue a track that seems not to have been well-traveled, namely to take very seriously the creative religious energy that the Wesleys invested in practices and to inquire into the theological import that might be imbedded in those practices. We will examine a distinctive subset of these Methodist practices, a subset that we term "Marks of Methodism," a subset that exhibits Methodism's way of being church, a subset that, we suggest, conveys its understanding of itself as church. The four marks or practices that we probe for their ecclesiological significance are itinerancy, discipline, connectionalism, and catholicity.

ix

We endeavor to depict each of these "marks" so as to exhibit as much of its Wesleyan nuance as possible and to draw out its religious and theological import. That idealization sets up the problematic of this approach. If the Wesleys and Methodism did imbed theology in practices, in marks, how should we theologically read the changes that practices inevitably undergo? Are they improvements? Are they declensions? Are they merely evolutions?

Our studies and those of others remind us that over time religious practices became complex, routinized, structured, detail-filled, politicized, and inertial. A case in point, as we shall show, was "discipline." This word American Methodists applied as title for the set of rules for holy living—the disciplines—that John Wesley prescribed for the people called Methodist. The action or verb character of "discipline," obvious in the terse, imperative quality of early editions, becomes much harder to grasp when the *Discipline* swells from the brief pamphlet of religious practices that it was after 1784 to the almost eight hundred pages that it requires now to specify the policies, structures, regulations, organizations, and offices for corporation-like United Methodism.

Such regimentation, formalization, or institutionalization, always a threat to the religious impulse, works double damage for Methodists. Most obviously, perhaps, institutionalization dampens piety or, as we would now term it, spirituality. Other movements or denominations more confessional or liturgical in character, equally vulnerable to the tendency to formalization, can look to their doctrines or worship as resource for guidance in renewal when organization and institution overwhelm their piety. Such churches—for instance, Lutherans, Presbyterians, or Anglicans—can appeal to the authority of creed, confession, or liturgy when their religious practices waver. Methodists, however, because they imbed doctrine as well as the religious impulse in practices, lack the easy appeal to external authority for renewal. When Methodist practices lose their vitality, so do, we suggest, the theology and ethics borne in the practices. At least that should be Methodism's worry.

So we ask, does the alteration, evolution, or atrophy of practices erode the church's theology and doctrine? If so, what might be undertaken as stratagems for revitalization? Will the altering of practices—including those incorporated into the organizational structure—will amending such practices or praxis produce renewal and revitalization? To date, efforts at reform that aim directly at United Methodist institutions and structures have produced ever-greater complexity—not renewal.

Not surprisingly, given how institutionalized have become our practices, our marks, Methodists have had great difficulty in claiming them for their theological import or perceiving them as a resource for renewal.

It has been hard, then, to make credible the theological and ethical import of our polity, of our practices. Exactly that we attempt here. The paragraphs that follow in this preface, however, detour from explicit attention to this thematic to describe the background and context of this inquiry into marks or practices and to delineate the studies, conferences, and publications that shape this volume's apparatus. Some readers may find it easier to jump to the introduction and, when engaged in the chapters that follow, to return to the preface for guidance on the short reference form we use.

UMAC

This volume is one of a series of publications deriving from research, consultations, and conferences undertaken under a major grant from the Lilly Endowment, Inc. and entitled **United Methodism and American Culture [UMAC].**

This five-year study was directed by Dennis M. Campbell and Russell E. Richey, both then at the Divinity School of Duke University. William B. Lawrence served as Project Associate. Counsel was provided by an Advisory Board composed of Jackson W. Carroll, Director of the Ormond Center, Duke University; Rosemary Skinner Keller, Dean of Union Theological Seminary, New York; Donald G. Mathews, Professor of History, University of North Carolina, Chapel Hill; Cornish R. Rogers, Professor of Pastoral Theology, Claremont School of Theology; and Judith Smith, Associate General Secretary, Office of Interpretation, General Board of Higher Education and Ministry, United Methodist Church.

The UMAC project began under a planning grant that made it possible for the principals (Campbell, Richey, and Lawrence) to engage in exploratory conversations with a wide array of church members, including board and agency leaders, bishops and district superintendents, clergy and laity, and United Methodist faculty as well as researchers in other Lilly-sponsored studies. From the counsel received through such exploratory discussions, the project came to pursue three primary objectives:

1. to provide a careful, fresh estimate of the history of Methodism in America, with particular attention to its twentieth century experience;
2. to attempt a portrait of United Methodism at the dawning of a new century;

3. to explore policy issues, with a view to the church's effective participation in American society and the world in the future.

We pursued those objectives through a variety of means: sponsored research; dialogue with the several internal commissions, committees, and projects studying United Methodism during the 1992–96 quadrennium; conversations with denominational executives; and a series of conferences and consultations. In the latter process, approximately seventy-five church leaders, scholars, and researchers participated, each working on a specific aspect, theme, or issue from the comprehensive task.

From their individual studies derived three Abingdon volumes of essays: *Connectionalism: Ecclesiology, Mission and Identity* (1997), *The People(s) Called Methodist: Forms and Reforms of Their Life* (1998), and *Doctrine and Discipline* (1999). These volumes thematically touched on all three of our objectives for the "United Methodism and American Culture" project but focused on the first two. The third objective was addressed by the three principals in a series of occasional papers entitled *Leadership Letters* and in a policy-oriented volume, *Questions for the Twenty-first Century Church* (1999), which posed and addressed questions facing the church at the dawn of the new century. Policy concerns ran through our conferences and gave rise to publications and proposals from others in our project in a variety of media and through legislative proposals laid before the General Conference of The United Methodist Church.

From the start of this project, Abingdon committed itself to be the "publisher of record" and to make the results appropriately accessible to United Methodism. As part of that commitment and this project, Abingdon has already published *The Methodist Conference in America* (Richey) and is publishing a two-volume collaborative effort (also involving Richey), *The Methodist Experience in America,* one volume of which will be narrative, the other a historical source book, already available.

Apparatus

The project culminates in this synthetic volume. To facilitate conversation with the research and researchers in our volumes, we have constructed a short-reference system. In Appendix I, we display the contents of each of the volumes, bolding within each title the abbreviation we employ for the individual article. After the full entry appears the abbreviation for author and essay title. We also offer an abbreviation for the volume title. So *Connectionalism: Ecclesiology, Mission, and Identity,* UMAC I, we abbreviate as (CEMI). The title and abbreviations for the essays appear in Appendix I as these two initial entries illustrate:

Introduction 1-20
Russell E. Richey
Richey, "Introduction," *CEMI*, 1-20

Connectionalism and Itinerancy:
Wesleyan Principles and Practice
Richard P. Heitzenrater 23-38
Heitzenrater, "Connectionalism and Itinerancy," *CEMI*, 23-38

Appendix II restates the abbreviations for United Methodism and American Culture, volumes I-IV, alphabetically by authors of the individual essays, along with a reminder of the abbreviations used for the volumes as a whole:

  I. *Connectionalism: Ecclesiology, Mission and Identity (CEMI)*
  II. *The People(s) Called Methodist: Forms and Reforms of Their Life (PCM)*
  III. *Doctrines and Discipline (DD)*
  IV. *Questions for the Twenty-First Century Church (QTCC)*

Becker, "Local Mission," *CEMI*, 267-85
Bell, "Homosexuality," *QTCC*, 271-79
Boomershine, "Electronic Culture," *QTCC*, 79-90
. . . .
Wright, "Public Education," *DD*, 179-95
Zech, "Funding Crisis," *CEMI*, 245-64
Zech, "Giving," *PCM*, 87-105.

These short-references then appear in our notes.

Appendix III indicates standardized abbreviations employed for church names, serials, and frequently used Methodist volumes.

Authorship

The three of us worked collaboratively on all the volumes edited to date, the lead name indicating which of us took primary responsibility in the editing process. For this synthetic effort we together identified the themes that ran through the UMAC research. We came to recognize, as well, how readily those themes clustered around what we came to call "Marks of Methodism," institutions or policies or ideational constructs that

- derive from the life and work of the Wesleys,
- have typified the Wesleyan religious impulse,
- characterize Methodism today, and
- retain the capacity, when understood afresh, to once again radi-
  ate Wesleyan convictions, values, beliefs, and hopes.

The three of us brainstormed about how each of those "marks" or practices might be treated and how they might be treated collectively so as (1)
to capture emphases of the UMAC research and (2) to provide a theological overview of Methodism. The case for such an appraisal of
Methodism we explore further in the introduction. Here we indicate that
though the approach, theme development, and outline were shared
endeavors, Richey assumes the blame for the crafting and drafting of the
introduction and the chapters that follow. Hence the title page and its
statement of authorship.

Acknowledgments

We gratefully acknowledge the several selections from *The Works of
John Wesley*, begun as The Oxford Edition of The Works of John Wesley
(Oxford: Clarendon Press, 1975–1983), continued as The Bicentennial
Edition of The Works of John Wesley (Nashville: Abingdon Press, 1984–),
especially the selections of hymns from volume 7. We also express appre-
ciation to the United Methodist News Service for the two releases:

PRESS RELEASE: Presented by Melvin G. Talbert, Resident Bishop.
Office of the Bishop, San Francisco Area of The United Methodist Church
at United Methodist Center West Sacramento, California, March 23,
1999—12:00 noon. Source: http://www.umc.org/umns/99/mar/157.htm.
Produced by United Methodist News Service. March 23, 1999 {157}.
Used with permission of UMNS.

and

United Methodist News Service {210}. Used with UMNS permission.
Green is news writer of UMNS's Nashville, Tenn., office. Source:
http://umc.org/umns/99/apr/210.htm. Paragraphing altered to suit
vignette format.

Russell E. Richey
Candler School of Theology
Emory University

Theology, Connection, and Practices
"What to Teach; How to Teach;
and What to Do"

The title of this volume is as old as the Wesleyan movement and apt for the very latest Methodist theological self-designation. "Marks of Methodism" points back to John Wesley himself and to his efforts to define the movement. It accurately and succinctly denotes how Methodists, under pressures from without or within, characterized and characterize themselves, namely in the conjunction of their theology, polity, and practices and in the embodiments or marks thereof.[1]

Identifying central and shared emphases constituted a Wesleyan strategy to hold the movement together, a strategy to bridge differences, a strategy to orient the people called Methodist. From early stages of American Methodism, naming the "marks" served efforts to sustain unity or overcome disunity. Mediating efforts between Methodist evangelicals and liberals today reach back to the same stratagem—claiming the common or shared emphases that transcend theological and programmatic differences.[2]

Such "marks" or hallmarks prescribe a basis for Methodist identity, purpose, unity. They also serve well to differentiate Methodists from other Christians, to sketch the boundaries of our movement, to mark us off. In addition, marks invite attention to the conjunction of precept and practice, to the considerable recent affirmation of practices as the traditioning and corporate bearers of Christian faithfulness and witness, and therefore as the ground of theology and doctrine, and to Methodist embodiment of and featuring of traditioning practices long before that became fashionable.[3]

In this volume, the marks evidence Methodist, particularly United Methodist, practices of church. They point to an understanding of church, a doctrine of the church, an ecclesiology embedded in the everyday structures, policies, organizations, and patterns of Methodist life.

Reading our book, a Methodist and particularly a United Methodist will discover that we have in our heritage—indeed, in our everyday experience—a vibrant, important, compelling practice of church.

1

Methodists have sometimes been taught the opposite—namely that we lack a doctrine of the church. We will invite the reader to consider that both claims may be true. A full-orbed, propositional, philosophically complex, and logically or intellectually rendered doctrine we may possibly lack. But a practiced or practical ecclesiology, a practical divinity on life together in the Spirit we have and have had. We will attempt to display instances of just such a practical ecclesiology and to identify some of its characteristics.

"The Marks of a True Methodist"

In several places Wesley attempted to delineate the several aspects of this "practical divinity." He did so, for instance, in the 1742 essay "The Character of a Methodist."[4] There he affirmed, "The distinguishing marks of a Methodist are not his opinions of any sort." He elaborated three other distinctives that are not characterizing and asked, "What then is the mark? Who is a Methodist, according to your own account?" and answers, "A Methodist is one who has 'the love of God shed abroad in his heart by the Holy Ghost given unto him.'" He then continued with a dozen marks, elaborating such entire dedication to God in scriptural phrasing:

> He is therefore happy in God. . . . Having found "redemption through his blood, the forgiveness of his sins," he cannot but rejoice. . . . He rejoiceth also, whenever he looks forward, "in hope of the glory that shall be revealed."

> From him, therefore, he cheerfully receives all, saying, "Good is the will of the Lord;". . . For he hath "learned, in whatsoever state he is, therewith to be content."

> [H]e "prays without ceasing."

> [T]his commandment is written in his heart, that "he who loveth God, loves his brother also."

> [H]e is "pure in heart."

> [T]he one design of his life is . . . "not to do his own will, but the will of Him that sent him."

> [A]s he loves God, so "he keeps his commandments."

> [L]oving God with all his heart, he serves him with all his strength. . . . All the talents he has received, he constantly employs according to his Master's will. . . .

[W]hatsoever he doeth, it is all to the glory of God.

Nor do the customs of the world at all hinder his "running the race that is set before him."

Lastly, as he has time, he "does good unto all men"—unto neighbours and strangers, friends and enemies. And that in every possible kind.

He concluded with two paragraphs, one of which begins, "These are the *principles* and *practices* of our SECT; these are the *marks* of a true Methodist." The second begins, "By these *marks*, by these fruits of a living faith, do we labour to *distinguish* ourselves from the unbelieving world, from all those whose minds or lives are not according to the gospel of Christ."

Marks as Descriptive and Unitive

In describing Methodism by its marks, by the fruits of a living faith, Wesley began a tradition of self-presentation that Methodists have followed to the very present. Wesley also created or claimed or reshaped practices—explicit mandates like the "General Rules" and institutionalized practices like love feast and itinerancy—by and through which the people called Methodist would offer and claim grace, and evidence the fruits of a living faith. His mandates, examples, provisions, structures, and processes for Christian living gradually gathered in and embodied the biblical virtues that he identified as "marks." And thereafter, Methodists sustained Christian faith, hope, and love, and maintained their Christian fidelity, integrity, and holiness by the marks or practices passed to them from Wesley.

So, not surprisingly, when Methodists have needed to gauge whether they were on course they sometimes turned, as did Wesley, to ask what characterizes or marks them off. A recent effort to discern the marks of Methodism came in the dialogue between liberal and evangelical wings of the denomination as they probed for grounds for unity. Sponsored by General Commission on Christian Unity and Interreligious Concerns in 1997 and 1998, the dialogue listed oft-cited concerns or points of disagreement, but also itemized points and practices of agreement. The marks noted in the United Methodist News Service (UMNS) release, which follows, might have been drafted at any number of stages in Methodist history:

NASHVILLE, Tenn. (UMNS)—First on the agenda of a dialogue on theological perspectives in the United Methodist Church here Nov. 20-21 was identification of factors that have created and preserved unity in the denomination and points of tension and difference that threaten to undermine that unity.

Points of unity, in no order of importance and with no approval by the entire group, included the following:

- connectionalism, including itineracy, episcopacy, institutional life, conferencing and common worship resources and sacraments;

- shared doctrinal and theological heritages;

- loyalty to denomination;

- personal piety and social holiness;

- Wesleyan distinctives or emphases;

- love of God;

- catholic spirit;

- evangelism and missions;

- Bible and role of scripture;

- inclusiveness;

- affirmation of laity;

- work of the Holy Spirit.[5]

At other points in Methodist or Wesleyan history, groups and individuals struggling to achieve or maintain unity have found it important to identify a list of characteristics or marks shared from a common heritage. For instance, in 1876, the Methodist Episcopal Church and the Methodist Episcopal Church, South searching for what might overcome the decades of enmity and recrimination and heal the wounds suffered in Civil War and from slavery found grounds for fraternity in the marks of Methodism:

> Distinctive features of profession and polity are bound up with the name of Episcopal Methodism. That form of Christian propagandism and ecclesiastical economy has peculiar elements of power and qualities of attraction that commend its efficiency in proclaiming a pure Gospel to the world. Its cardinal doctrines of free salvation by faith, and of the witness of the Spirit; its scriptural articles of Christian belief; its primitive system of Church government; its sententious demand of those who would join its societies; its itinerant plan of preaching the Gospel, its

Wesleyan simplicity and orthodoxy; its urgency of the practice of a holy life; its liberal and systematic benevolence; its support of educational institutions; its promotion of Sabbath-school instruction; its vigilant care for the deserving poor; its provision for superannuated ministers, their widows and children; its worldwide missionary enterprise; and its general activity in the dissemination of Gospel truth, are one and the same in the Methodist Episcopal Church and in the Methodist Episcopal Church, South.[6]

This Cape May declaration began the long road to the unification achieved in 1939.[7] Similar enumerations and listings and celebrations of the essentials or characteristics of Methodism recur through the speeches and sermons at what now we know as the World Methodist Conference, the first also in 1876, and can be experienced in their published *Proceedings*.[8] Marks served prescriptive and unitive purposes.

Valuable as a resource for unity and concord, the marks of Methodism also function for interpretive or descriptive purposes. One such presentation of Methodism by its marks came soon after the 1939 union in *Methodism*, edited by William K. Anderson.[9] That volume identified the following as "Distinctive Emphases" of Methodism and devoted a chapter to each:

> Salvation for All
> God Can Be Experienced
> Freedom from Rigid Creed
> The Search for Perfection
> A Singing Church
> The Itinerant Ministry
> Methodism's Educational Activities
> Methodism's Contribution to Social Reform
> Methodism's World Parish

Bishops and other leaders employ their list of Methodist essentials or marks to encourage or exhort continued faithfulness, for instance, William C. Martin in 1948 before the Nebraska Conference or Gerald Kennedy in *The Marks of a Methodist*, which he identified in chapter titles as Experience, Results, Discipline, Mission, Freedom, and Perfection.[10] More recently, Mary Elizabeth Moore identified the "Marks of United Methodist Theology" as sixfold: practical, disciplined, fluid and constant, connectional, broad, and universally-minded.[11] Kenneth H. Carter, Jr. identified six practices that characterize or should characterize Wesleyan spirituality: Searching the Scriptures, Generosity with the

Poor, Testimony, Singing, Holy Communion, and Life Together.[12] Similar thematically structured portrayals of Methodist marks have appeared from time to time.[13] Indeed, one such depiction is issued every four years. The official version of such marks can now be found in the prefatory matter in the Discipline—Constitution, Doctrine and Doctrinal Statements, General Rules, and Social Principles.

United Methodism and American Culture

In this volume, we presume on this tradition of authoritative Methodist self-presentations, represented preeminently by the *Discipline* though not, of course, claiming such authority for our effort. We suggest that "Marks of Methodism" enable us to pull together recent research on United Methodism and American culture.[14] Our own research and that of others have reclaimed, enlivened, enriched, deepened, and nuanced the practices/principles that have been marks or hallmarks of Methodist identity and of Methodist self-presentation from the days of Wesley. Attempting to discover deeper patterns in this research, we found ourselves beginning to do what Methodists have done through the decades when they would identify themselves and their movement. We and they have characterized Methodism not with a tight creedal or confessional affirmation but with an array of characteristics embracing belief, practice, ethos, commitment, lifestyle, and mission.[15]

In our first endeavor to summarize our own work and that of our many others, we also gradually discerned a similar master list and identified the following marks of Methodism:

Scriptural	Arminian
Episcopal	Sacramental
Holy	Reforming/Forming
Oral/Aural	Evangelical/Missionary
Itinerant	Disciplined
Connectional	Catholic/Uniting

These marks, which figure in one or more of the preceding lists, seemed to us to catch up historic and continuing Wesleyan commitments and practices, commitments and practices that remain essential for United Methodism today. Other interpreters, depending on their focus and purpose, doubtless might offer additional marks or seek a shorter list, some of the above subsumed therein. These we judged would provide an overview of Methodism.

Marks of Methodism: Practices of Ecclesiology

Treating the full list of marks, examining each mark at an appropriate depth, and covering Methodism as a whole, both present and past, will be a task for us in the near future, but a big task. Would a subset of these, we asked, lend themselves to characterizing the whole and particularly in epitomizing Methodist life together? Would a few marks adequately capture themes of our own studies, which have focused on the Methodist connection, on Methodism in its institutional expressions, on Methodism as one manifestation of the Body of Christ? We concluded that treating a subset of the above would indeed

- allow us to explore distinctive Wesleyan practices, and practices that cohere and interrelate as an enacted ecclesiology;
- exhibit essential Wesleyan concerns that prove most important in relating United Methodism to or separating it from other Christian movements;
- permit us most easily to illustrate how such marks have functioned, where they have changed through the course of Methodist history, and what parts they play in United Methodist life today;
- provide an opportunity to pull together themes and findings from recent research including our own and that which we have sponsored.[16]

Four marks, we judge, characterize Methodist practices of church, notably, connectional, disciplined, catholic, and itinerant.[17]

Connectional, disciplined, catholic, and itinerant—these four Methodist marks—serve well to epitomize Methodism, particularly Methodist life together. And they link nicely and appropriately with what have been traditionally termed the "notes" or "marks" of the church, classic affirmations Christians make about the nature and purpose of the church. The church is one, holy, catholic, and apostolic. Individually and collectively these traditional ecclesial affirmations parallel the four Methodist marks.

Methodism's connectionalism, we suggest, points to the oneness of the church. Its discipline points to holiness. Its catholic spirit clearly points to catholicity. And its itinerancy, we will show, points to apostolicity. These marks, then, illustrate how Methodists embed fundamental Christian affirmations in practices; how Methodists practice what the church, ecumenically and traditionally, has preached about itself; how

Methodists do doctrine; how Methodists dramatize in their collective life the classic notes of the church.

Further, these four Wesleyan marks—connectional, disciplined, catholic, and itinerant—as ecclesial practices require attention to other marks in our list above. Several of the other marks, we suggest, can and should be embraced by the four we examine or represent practices to which the above four point.

Connectionalism had and has the mark of forming and reforming as one of its mandates, an imperative clearly expressed in the American version of Wesley's command "to reform the continent, and spread scripture-holiness over these lands" [the phrasing in the *Discipline*, variously placed]. Discipline, though its associations today might not suggest it, had fundamentally to do with the ends—individual and corporate—for which we were created, ends captured by hallmark Wesleyan insistence on holiness or perfection. The term *catholic* readily embraces that which symbolizes and actualizes unity in Christ, namely the sacraments. *Itinerant* points to the teaching and general superinten-ding office, which in Methodist understanding models and makes itinerancy feasible, the episcopacy or, as we have understood the office, "itinerant general superintendency." Four other marks, then—reforming/forming, holy, sacramental, and episcopal—closely relate to the four marks treated here: connectional, disciplined, catholic/uniting, and itinerant. We might understand the values to ecclesiology and visualize these interrelations of the "Marks of Methodism" accordingly:

Connectional	Reforming/Forming	One
Disciplined	Holy	Holy
Catholic/Uniting	Sacramental	Catholic
Itinerant	Episcopal	Apostolic

The other four Wesleyan marks—oral/aural, evangelical/missionary, scriptural, and Arminian—shape and form all the marks (including each other) as styles or patterns of Methodist testifying, conveying, knowing, and apprehending. First, treating the eight marks above requires us to indicate that Methodist beliefs and practices have been transmitted orally and aurally by preaching, singing, praying, and testifying. Second, the eight marks became Methodist practices through the aggressive, soul-saving witness—a witness that shaped what conveyed its own mold, namely as an evangelical/missionary ecclesial style. Third, and most important, adequately treating the eight and the four focused upon here, turns us to the scriptural warrants to which the marks point, graphically indicated in Wesley's enumerated list. And, fourth, to examine these four involves us in developing the Arminian theology, the evangelical doctrines, in terms of which the Wesleys understood the biblical witness.[18] So do the oral/aural, evangelical/missionary, scriptural, and Arminian marks in Methodist practice of Christian living.

These last four marks shape and form all the marks insofar as they work to give expression to a fourfold way of presenting, conveying, knowing, and apprehending, which the next sections examine and which we illustrate in this fashion:

Oral/Aural	[Tradition]
Evangelical/Missionary	[Experience]
Scriptural	[Scripture]
Arminian	[Reason]

These four marks represent the way in which what we now term the quadrilateral worked itself out in Methodist life. A few notes are in order.

A Tradition of Singing

Associating tradition with testifying, putting it as "oral/aural," and arranging it first in the above listing and in the chapters that follow may not seem the most obvious and most readily warranted identification and placement. That equation/location we will find useful in this volume for the clarity with which it permits us to show how our traditions of preaching, singing, praying and testifying have shaped us as a movement.[19] To illustrate each mark we begin with a Charles Wesley hymn, and we have deliberately selected ones that lie outside our present repertoire. We make the choices to point to a rich lode of Wesleyan theology not readily mined. When we sang primarily from a larger range of Wesley verse, we readily voiced fundamental Wesleyan commitments, values, beliefs, and aspirations. Singing traditioned us as did the other oral/aural ways of proclaiming Wesleyan doctrine—preaching, praying, testifying, and writing. A lovefeast hymn like the following richly conveys the major emphases of this volume, and we will draw on selected hymns to help us understand each of the four marks treated here:

1 LET us join, ('tis God commands)[20]
Let us join our hearts and hands
Help to gain our calling's hope,
Build we each the other up:

God his blessings shall dispense,
God shall crown his ordinance;
Meet in his appointed ways;
Nourish us with social grace.

2 Let us then as brethren love,
Faithfully his gifts improve,
Carry on the earnest strife,
Walk in holiness of life;
Still forget the things behind,
Follow Christ in heart and mind,
Toward the mark unwearied press,
Seize the crown of righteousness.

3 Plead we thus for faith alone,
Faith which by our works is shown:
God it is who justifies;
Only faith the grace applies;
Active faith that lives within,
Conquers earth, and hell, and sin,
Sanctifies, and makes us whole,
Forms the Saviour in the soul.

4 Let us for this faith contend,
Sure salvation is its end:
Heaven already is begun,
Everlasting life is won.
Only let us persevere,
Till we see our Lord appear,
Never from the rock remove,
Saved by faith, which works by love.

Hymns do keep us in touch with our Wesleyan tradition. One could wish that more effort were made to reclaim Charles Wesley's hymns and to set them to singable tunes. But why begin with a hymn rather than a biblical text? Why tradition first and not Scripture?

"What to Teach; How to Teach; and What to Do"

The title of this introduction recalls the guiding imperative employed by John Wesley when he convened the first conferences. It points to three concerns of the volume as a whole—theology, connection, and practices. And it reminds us that we need to respect their conjunction if we would accurately describe our movement, now or in the past. Within the context of conference (connection) and through the modality of conference (conversations), Mr. Wesley sought to refine the teachings *(theology)* and duties and disciplines (practices) of the infant movement. The "how" of teaching and duty Wesley examined in the conference itself, embodied in the various communal structures and processes, outlined in the *Minutes* (our *Discipline*), and thereby defined and characterized Methodist polity and practice.

Wesley's formulation "What to teach; How to teach; and What to do; that is, how to regulate our doctrine, discipline, and practice"[21] has helped guide Methodists into holding principles and practice together. We routinely affirm that Wesley was not a systematic theologian in the fashion of Catholic scholastics and Protestant Reformers. Rather he provided an experimental or practical theology. But his was a theology with its own coherence, integrity, method, as we have been taught from the mid-twentieth century onward by George Croft Cell, William R. Cannon, Colin W. Williams, Albert Outler, Martin Schmidt, Frank Baker, and others. And the Wesley *Works* project has continued to fuel and be fueled by explorations into the Wesleys and their theology. And yet despite the ongoing affirmation of the practical character of Wesley's theology, despite the recent emphases on practices, and despite the continuing honor to the adage, attributed to Prosper of Aquitaine, *lex orandi, lex credendi*, we seem tempted to move only in one way through Wesley's formulation—from what to teach to what to do. The common move is from precept, theology, and text to practice, polity, and practical application. First Wesleyan doctrine is established, and then its expression follows in life and work.[22]

Surprisingly there seems to be little inclination among Methodists to go the other way, from the practices and polity of Methodism to their theological meaning.[23] Hymnody and our singing might be cited as the exception. From the very first our hymns and hymnbooks functioned, as Charles and John Wesley prescribed, as "a little body of experimental and practical divinity," and provided a lyric version of the marks of Methodism. Indeed, beginning in 1780 the Wesleys structured the *Collection of Hymns for the Use of the People Called Methodists* as a pathway to salvation, a Methodist guide to living the Christian life. For several decades American hymnals preserved the soteriological Wesleyan formatting. Even without that structure and through the years, the Wesleyan hymns have been identified as bearer of our Methodist doctrine (even as each new hymnal omitted successively more of them).[24] But here, too, the text rather than the practice typically commands attention. While the actual singing, the choices and use of hymns, and their place in the faith of the believer would be, of course, more difficult to capture, might not such practices deserve the greater attention?

This work endeavors to move the other way across Wesley's queries— from "what to do," through "how to do," to "what to teach." So we begin each chapter with a hymn and some probing of the mark, a discussion that leads then into a vignette, an actual portrayal of Methodist life, of Methodism at work, of Methodist practice. Originally we planned to narrate those vignettes, but we worried that we might be accused of setting up the theological commentary and analysis that followed. So the vignettes come out of American Methodist experience. Some reach back in time. Others are more contemporary. Each, along with the hymn, permits us to begin with Methodist practices and to discover therein layers of theological import, a far richer theological life than we as a movement typically receive credit for or even credit ourselves for.[25] So far, then, with hymn and vignette we actualize two parts of the quadrilateral: tradition and experience.

Marks and Pietism: Christian Experience

We are mindful that the title of the volume and the discussion so far derive from Wesley and the specifically Methodist, rather than from the Evangelical United Brethren (EUB), wing of the heritage. We select the title because, while its allusion is specific, it is faithful to the larger evangelical tradition in which United Brethren, Evangelicals, and Methodists stand. The phrasing does indeed come from John Wesley rather than from William Otterbein, Martin Boehm, or Jacob Albright. However, the phrasing captures a typical Pietist or evangelical concern: to highlight those aspects of Christian practice, ethos, ethic, and belief that bind believers together rather than to focus on those doctrinal or liturgical distinctives that separate.[26]

Pietist and pietist-like movements characteristically put emphasis on

- experimental religion, locating the religious impulse in the heart (will and affections);
- both consciousness and expression of the heart's commitments (conversion and testimony);
- an obedient life, strict moral codes, and corporate discipline as appropriate expressions thereof;

- the accessibility of the biblical word and rule to the awakened lay spirit;
- growth in the faith through active devotions but also through education, educational programs, and literature, all adjusted to suit age, culture, and circumstance;
- the importance of a witness communally shared through prayer, Bible-reading, hymns, and preaching;
- everyday life as a sacrament to be shaped and enlivened by a vibrant faith and expressed in holy living; and
- doctrine or doctrines as the light by which all this activism stays on course.

Recognizing the marks of these Pietist commitments in each other's lives made it possible for William Otterbein and Martin Boehm to recognize the other as brother. So also they could discern the marks of genuine Christianity in Francis Asbury and his English-speaking colleagues. Marks was Wesley's word, but the practices to which it pointed and the discernment of spirits that resulted characterized the larger Pietist impulse.

Quadrilateral Again: Scripture and Reason

Since its appearance, thanks to Albert Outler, in the 1972 *Discipline* as *the* Wesleyan theological method,[27] the quadrilateral has prompted both controversy and appreciation. Though its critics remain, its central place in United Methodist intellectual life seems, for now, to have been safeguarded by the 1988 Disciplinary refinement acknowledging the primacy of Scripture but retaining quadrilateral as the Methodist system of authority.[28] However, if the value of the quadrilateral can be read through Board of Ordained Ministry interviews, one might conclude that it is more important to acknowledge the quadrilateral and insist on the primacy of Scripture therein than actually to make use of it in parish theological formulation, preaching, or teaching.

This work endeavors to make the quadrilateral an operative methodology, a way of doing theology, not itself a doctrine to be subscribed. The subtitle of this chapter clues its importance. The first and third in these two triads:

Theology, Connection, and Practices
"What to Teach; How to Teach; and What to Do"

point clearly to reason and experience. "Connection" and "How to Teach" can provide us opportunity to reference tradition, primarily in its

Methodist expression. But what of Scripture? How do we discern its guidance and safeguard its primacy? Instead of beginning each chapter with a vignette (experience), why not start the exploration of these marks with Scripture? That certainly would be an acceptable way to proceed. Indeed, Wesley's own delineation of marks does, at first reading, seem to move from Scripture to description. But, note that Wesley reaches to Scripture to describe the living faith of Methodists. His is not a simple movement from precept to practice, from text to application, from doctrine to life. Such a one-directional intellectual movement, from Scripture to theology to practice, would trace the scholastic and systematic procedure. That one-directional movement characterized Calvinist or Reformed divines against whom Wesley struggled.

A Wesleyan engagement with Scripture moves back and forth, from life to Scripture and from Scripture to life, enriching the reading as Scripture writes itself on the heart, and deepening the spirituality as the heart rereads Scripture. These hermeneutical moves, to be authentic and faithful, must indeed be guided by the Spirit and undertaken prayerfully. They involve the heart. They also involve the head. Scripture and reason interplay in complex and complementary fashion.

So a Methodist intellectual movement need not begin with Scripture to honor its primacy. Indeed, one might argue that only a weak doctrine of the Word equates it with the text of Scripture. Would not more adequate doctrines of revelation and inspiration claim the eternal Word, and the Word preached, and the Word of Scripture; insist on encounter with each; and demand a hermeneutic that moves with the Spirit through the several hearings?[29]

So when a sermon begins with some personal or corporate experience one cannot, by that starting point, presume that the Methodist preacher has begun somewhere else than with Scripture, with the Word. Rather she may indeed have begun on her knees with the Word—with the living Word that shapes her life and work. And that living Word has been conveyed to her through study, reflection, and prayer—engagement with the scriptural Word. And the Word will be conveyed to the congregation through lively, effective preaching, guided by the Spirit, which is reason employed soteriologically. Scripture's primacy entails and requires a living Word conveyed through preaching that was itself grounded intimately, diligently, and faithfully in the Word made flesh in Christ, and conveyed to us in Holy Scripture. So we will pursue Scripture through the exploration of the entirety of each mark and end, rather than begin, our chapters with a scriptural summary.

Doctrine and Theology

By proceeding in this inductive, interactive fashion and looking at the marks of Methodism as they emerge in the life, structure, and processes of the movement, we endeavor indeed to hold together doctrine, theology, connection, and practices. And we hold together tradition, experience, Scripture, and reason. This approach honors the dynamic, processional, pneumatological, teleological character of "Our Theological Task" (*Discipline*, Para. 104, Section 4). True to our Wesleyan heritage, Methodists have enacted and teased out our theology in a processional, goal-oriented, missional fashion. We have acted and thought toward holiness, social and personal. Our theological endeavor, when true to its sources, has been not static but processional. By examining marks we exhibit Methodism undertaking its theological task.

The approach, however, does not lead away from doctrine, from what the church has taught and holds as normative.[30] Indeed, the converse emerges. By attending closely to what Methodists, at their best, do in fidelity to their traditions, we find the doctrines of creed and confession graphically writ in Methodist practices. "Connectional, disciplined, catholic, and itinerant," these our marks serve well to characterize Methodism, particularly Methodist life together. These characteristic practices point through authentic Methodism to the traditional notes or marks of the church. Methodism's connectionalism affirms the oneness of the church, its discipline holiness, its catholic spirit catholicity, and its itinerancy apostolicity. So the reader may expect to find here "the common fundamental principles of Christianity":

> These are the principles and practices of our sect; these are the marks of a true Methodist. By these alone do those who are in derision so called desire to be distinguished from other men. If any man say, "Why, these are only the common fundamental principles of Christianity!"—"Thou has said. So I mean. This is the very truth. I know they are no other, and I would to God both thou and all men knew that I, and all who follow my judgment, do vehemently refuse to be distinguished from other men by any but the common principles of Christianity—the plain, old Christianity that I teach, renouncing and detesting all other marks of distinction.[31]

CHAPTER ONE

Connectional

1 BLEST be the dear uniting love,[1]
That will not let us part!
Our bodies may far off remove,
We still are one in heart.

2 Joined in one spirit to our Head,
Where he appoints we go;
And still in Jesu's footsteps tread,
And show his praise below.

3 O may we ever walk in him,
And nothing know beside;
Nothing desire, nothing esteem,
But Jesus crucified.

4 Closer and closer let us cleave
To his beloved embrace;
Expect his fulness to receive
And grace to answer grace.

5 Partakers of the Saviour's grace,
The same in mind and heart,
Nor joy, nor grief, nor time, nor place,
Nor life, nor death can part.

6 But let us hasten to the day
Which shall our flesh restore,
When death shall all be done away,
And bodies part no more!

"Connectionalism," to the average United Methodist, suggests machinery—apportionments, boards and agencies, hierarchy, conference headquarters, the church's officialdom, its apparatus. Such a perception is neither inappropriate nor new. The image of Methodism as machine runs deep in our consciousness and our heritage. When

Bishops Francis Asbury and Thomas Coke annotated the *Discipline* and explained the church to American society in 1798, they referred to Methodism as a machine. They insisted on the necessity of preserving "in order and in motion the wheels of the vast machine."[2] Not half a century later George Cookman (then chaplain to the Senate), soon to be lost at sea, drew upon Ezekiel's image of wheels within wheels to interpret Methodism.

> The *great iron wheel* in the system is *itinerancy*, and truly it grinds some of us most tremendously; the *brazen wheel*, attached and kept in motion by the former, is the *local ministry*; the *silver wheel*, the *class leaders*; and *golden wheel*, the *doctrine and discipline of the church*, in full and successful operation. Now, sir, it is evident that the entire movement depends upon keeping the *great iron wheel of itinerancy* constantly and rapidly rolling around. But, to be more specific, and to make an application of this figure to American Methodism. Let us carefully note the admirable and astounding movements of this wonderful machine. You will perceive there are "wheels within wheels." First, there is the great outer wheel of episcopacy, which accomplishes its entire revolution *once in four years*. To this there are attached *twenty-eight smaller wheels*, styled *annual conferences*, moving around *once a year*; to these are attached *one hundred wheels*, designated *presiding elders*, moving twelve *hundred other wheels*, termed *quarterly conferences*, every *three* months; to these are attached *four thousand wheels*, styled *travelling preachers*, moving round *once a month*, and communicating motion to *thirty thousand* wheels, called *class leaders*, moving round *once a week*, and who, in turn, being attached to between *seven and eight hundred thousand wheels*, called *members*, give a sufficient impulse to whirl them round *every* day. O, sir, what a machine is this! This is the machine of which Archimedes only dreamed; this is the machine destined, under God, to *move the world, to turn it upside down.*[3]

Throughout the nineteenth century, Methodists prided themselves on the machinelike quality of Methodism. Indeed, they equated the church with a machine. Abel Stevens, the MEC's midcentury historian and apologist, suggested that two machines conquered the American wilderness: the steam engine invented by James Watt and the moral engine invented by John Wesley.[4] Of the two, Methodism was truly "the machine in the garden."[5] In imaging itself as machine, indeed glorifying its machinelike qualities, Methodism clearly drew on a socially powerful metaphor of the day. The machine—steam and then internal combustion—made the industrial society. Methodism's connectionalism, our nineteenth century ancestors thought, functioned to make the church work with high efficiency, productivity, and creativity.

In the early twentieth century, Methodists spent less energy glorifying the Methodist machinery and more in making it run efficiently.[6] Efficiency, they believed, could be gained by collaboration, structure, procedure. So Paul Kern of the MECS, faculty member at Southern Methodist University and later bishop, and Worth Tippy of the MEC, Executive Secretary of the Church and Social Service Commission of the Federal Council of Churches, collaborated on a training manual for church leaders. There they explained connectionalism and then its machine character:

> Methodism is essentially connectional. . . .
> There are many denominations in which the connectional idea is not as strong as it is in Methodism. We regard it as a vital part of our ecclesiastical life. All the scattered and varied congregational groups are in reality parts of one splendid unity called Methodism. . . . Note how we stress our connectional idea. When a young man joins the ministry of our church he does not join any local Conference, he is a member of the world-wide fellowship of Methodist preachers, liable for service anywhere; our bishops are bishops of the whole church; our great objectives, such as missions and education, are handled through connectional boards, whose relationships are church wide. Whenever Methodism loses its confidence in the power of connectionalism, it will be almost certain to enter a career of disintegration.[7]

Their chapter titles capture the machinelike character of connectionalism: Our Heritage, The Purpose and Program of the Modern Church, Building the Christian Fellowship, The Church Organized for Worship, The Church Organized for Teaching, The Church Organized for Social Service, Making the Church Organization Efficient, Efficiency through General Organization, The Local Church in World-Wide Enterprise, Housing the Local Church, Financing the Local Church, Leadership.

And, of course, prominent in the efficiency revolution were apportionments.[8] If connectionalism is machinery, what keeps it humming is money. And if machinery and money constitute Methodism's character, both find fullest expression in their twentieth-century developments— bureaucracy and apportionments. So Methodism incarnated the ethos and forms of capitalism.

But do such images capture all of what we would say about connection or connectionalism? On the contrary, "connection" has and has had deeply spiritual and profoundly theological resonances. Many of these can be discerned in a recent event.

Vignette

Women's Congress:
A Journey in Spiritual and Leadership Development

Story by Linda Green

NORCROSS, Ga. (UMNS),[9] April 21, 1999—Tears of joy and release were the norm as more than 135 women gathered for five days to hear God's call in their lives. The diverse participants, described as "journey takers," came to United Methodist-related Simpsonwood Retreat Center near Atlanta to participate in the Women's Congress, April 14-18. It was a time of spiritual renewal and empowerment, leadership development and relationship building, aimed at preparing the group to serve the United Methodist Church and their communities more effectively.

The women—both lay and clergy—came from the United States and Puerto Rico to hear the message of sisterhood, to be reminded of examples taught to them by their foremothers in the faith, and to learn that women have offered their gifts to the church for centuries. They shared their personal and spiritual stories through writing, singing, chanting, dancing, praying and hands-on mission work. From clergywomen Janet Wolf, Linda Thomas, Grace Imathiu, Teresa Fry Brown and Naomi Southard, the participants learned lessons about who they are, the importance of storytelling, the nature of God's love and self-love, and the biblical stories of women. Other leaders included Donna Fado Ivery, Kappitola Williams, Cynthia Wilson Felder, Lydia S. Martinez, Heather Wood and Susan Peek.

The participants were reminded of how God's love and their love for God will initiate numerous possibilities for their lives, no matter what obstacles arise. Because of that love, the women were encouraged to remember the phrase that became an anthem at the congress: "And I'm Going On Anyhow." Thomas, a professor at Garrett Evangelical Theological School in Evanston, Ill., affirmed the women as created in God's image and following in God's way. "We came to listen to God speak to us, and we expect an answer," she said.

The importance of storytelling was stressed by both Wolf, pastor at Hobson United Methodist Church in Nashville, Tenn., and Imathiu, a doctoral candidate at Vanderbilt Divinity School, also in Nashville. Stories are critical and grounding, Imathiu said. "They give a beginning into conversations with each other and God. Each story is an entry point to the biblical story, God's story." As the women listened to Brown, they charted a course through the Bible looking at stories of women and how they had made the decision to follow God or to help their people.

The congress was conceived in 1995, when members of the churchwide Commission on the Status and Role of Women (COSROW) expressed the need for women to understand where God is calling them to be. "The church needs again and again to call forth women leaders—diverse women who will engage in a time of personal and spiritual growth," the congress design team said. The congress was described as an empowerment tool for women who are often overlooked for leadership positions in their local church settings. In 1998, letters were sent to more than 6,000 women in church-related leadership positions, requesting that each nominate a woman with leadership potential who would benefit from a Women's Congress. Participants reflected the diversity of women in the United Methodist Church in terms of race, ethnicity, age, theology, economics, geography, congregational size, rural, urban and suburban perspectives.

"To see such diversity in the room makes my soul sing with gladness," said congress Chairwoman Ethel Johnson of Columbus, Ohio. The congress was held because "we believe in the message that women are loved, gifted, precious creations of God," said the Rev. Stephanie Hixon, one of COSROW's two top executives. The congress invited women who may not always hear that message to know it, be deepened by it and celebrate it in their lives, she said. "We are here to encourage them in whatever way God is calling them in their lives."

Traveling was a special treat for most of the women. Some took their first airplane ride to attend the congress. Elizabeth "Pooh" Triplett, 18, a high school senior from Joplin, Mo., sacrificed her senior prom in order to attend the congress. "If I'd gone, I'd be with the same people I see every day," she said. When she reunites with her friends, "I'm going to tell them that while you were dancing in those high-heeled shoes and suffering from aching feet, I was conversing with women from around the world and learning their cultures." Triplett was one of three young women between 18 and 25 years old attending the congress.

After witnessing the unity of the highly diverse group of participants, Tamara Isidore of Tampa, Fla., said, "I've learned that I didn't have to die to enjoy heaven." The congress was designed to take the women on a spiritual journey, and to help them navigate around the church and learn of the numerous resources available to assist them, said Cecelia Long, another top COSROW executive. Hands-on work was part of the journey, Long said. "It is part of understanding how we relate to others." In 13 groups, the women fanned out to perform work at mission sites across Atlanta. They cleaned, sorted clothes, fed children and adults, stocked food pantries, worked at schools and a homeless shelter, and attended sites to listen to battered women and to hear stories from those suffering with AIDS.

Nitza Gomez of Orlando, Fla., expressed pride that, at the congress, racial differences vanished. "We are all one," she said. "I am a beloved daughter of God and a beloved sister of all of you." Any concern that she would feel out of place at the congress vanished for Mary Lou Segouia of Chamblee, Ga., when she began to hear the stories of other participants. When her pastor invited her to go, she said she felt like Moses—inadequate for the challenge—and suggested someone else be sent. "I'm glad I came because the experience has been awesome." Women need a place in the church, said Hildelisa Ordaz of Miami. "I am so proud to be in this event. We are pioneers. This will be history." Johnnie M. Robinson of Hugo, Okla., said she had planned to attend the meeting and quietly observe. That plan vanished after "I saw the movement of the Holy Spirit in this place." After her mission experience working with children, she realized that God is calling her toward that kind of work, she said. "The empty place inside has been filled," she said. "I now know what I am supposed to be doing."

Two members of the Christ Church of the Deaf in Washington were also awed by the level of inclusion at the congress. "I came to see what the United Methodist Church had for women," said LaSander Saunders of Owings Mills, Md. She expressed appreciation for translators, telephone devices and lights that blink when there is a knock at the door. "The women here touched me," said Norma Adams, the other deaf member. "God was here moving among all of us, and that touched my heart." Many women received a new understanding and appreciation for sign language when Saunders and Adams signed the Lord's Prayer, as the words were spoken by translators.

The breaking down of barriers was apparent during exchanges between Sharon Leas, a white woman from Dallas Center, Iowa, and Danita Page, a black woman from Little Rock, Ark. "It was great to understand that when we all get to heaven, we will be part of the same choir," Leas said. "It's been an experience to look in my sisters' eyes and learn," Page said. "I cannot return home to say 'them' again."

Commentary

Do machinery and money sum up connectionalism or are they but its instrumentalities? If one had to select a few words to capture this mark we term "connectional," would bureaucracy and apportionments best capture its meaning? Or might not gathering, festival, and expressiveness (hymns, praise, prayer, testimony) also be required? Indeed, might they serve better? And might the Women's Congress image Methodist connectionalism as much as or more than an agency meeting or conference headquarters? Yes, indeed! Marking Methodism in such conferencelike fashion also runs deep in our consciousness and heritage.

Jesse Lee—missionary to New England, chaplain to both House and Senate, Methodism's first historian, an almost-bishop—observed the annual conference of 1782 held at Ellis's Chapel, in Sussex County, Virginia. He noted:

> The union and brotherly love which I saw among the preachers, exceeded every thing I had ever seen before, and caused me to wish that I was worthy to have a place amongst them. When they took leave of each other, I observed that they embraced each other in their arms, and wept as though they never expected to meet again. Had the heathens been there, they might have well said, "see how the Christians love one another!" By reason of what I saw and heard during the four days that the conference sat, I found my heart truly humbled in the dust, and my desires greatly increased to love and serve God more perfectly than I had ever done before.[10]

Tears of joy and sorrow "oiled" the inner workings of the Methodist "machine"—its conferences, annual and quarterly, and its class meetings.[11] Through them, early American Methodism connected, did its business, deployed its leaders for mission. Much like the Women's Congress, early conferences gathered Methodists in all their diversity—leaders and laity, women and men, black and white, young and old, English and non-English-speaking for festival and business, praise and discipline, community and order.[12] Emotions and order went together.

Conference, quarterly meeting, or class exercised discipline and then sang, shouted, prayed, witnessed in love feast.[13] The Charles Wesley hymn with which this chapter begins sums up connectionalism nicely:

> BLEST be the dear uniting love,
> That will not let us part!
> Our bodies may far off remove,
> We still are one in heart.

Perhaps the *first* point to note about connectionalism, then, hinges on its conference or conferencelike character.[14] In a gathering, an event, a happening, an occasion for greeting and meeting, an invitation to spontaneity, a time for joy and sorrow,

Methodists connect and are connected.
They discover one another and themselves.
They recognize who they are as children of God.
They claim and renegotiate a Methodist identity.
They look out to the boundaries of the movement and in to its heart.
They find themselves in the longer story of God's people.
They re-experience the joys and tragedies of the human saga.

Story-telling indeed holds it together. It does so in a Women's Congress. It did so in the class or quarterly meeting or annual conference. In the sharing, in hearing another talk of her walk, in the relation-building, conferences and congresses functioned as means of grace in the way that John Wesley intended.[15] Connectionalism has to do with conferencing and our theology of connectionalism exhibits itself in our polity.[16] It is **first**, then, a *theology in praxis* or *theology of praxis.* And it is a theology of praxis as loving community or community of love. At points it may appear, indeed may be, a love of the connection, a love of the institution, a love of the machine. That, however, attests to its praxis character and the conjunction of means and ends. Methodists might love connection insofar as they actualize a community of love.

Understanding connectionalism in this conferencelike, festival, affectionate, narrative way points us to both the quality of the unity within Methodism and to the reality of a unity more broadly shared within the Christian family, indeed within the whole family of God. A community genuinely bound together in the love of Christ knows no boundaries imposed out of human frailties.

Such conferencelike, narrated community occurs in great gatherings like the Women's Congress. It occurs and has occurred more frequently and intensely in the smaller gatherings for which Wesleyanism has been so famous. Their shared testimony creates community and community lives off testimony. As a facet of Methodist life well-institutionalized in the love feast and class meeting, reconstituted in the Sunday school, and reshaping itself in various small groupings, the narrative and testimony-bonded community builds community from the bottom up. Often the bonds followed lines of age, gender, race, language, ethnicity—what Robert Putnam has termed "bonded social capital," that is "affinity-based." Occasionally, and in places, Methodism has been able to sustain in the small group what the Women's Congress achieved, namely what Putnam terms "bridging social capital," community despite real differences.[17] Either way, Methodist connectionalism has built itself on strong local networks.

Because Methodists act out their theology, because their manner and mode of connecting actualize basic commitments, the quality and character of gatherings matter. So, we argue elsewhere and strenuously that United Methodism needs to be more deliberate and careful about how and where it meets, about the size and style of its official gatherings, about how program uses time, about the drama and staging of the meeting, about who must attend, about how leaders lead. Too long, we suggest, have function and efficiency taken away the "joy and release."[18] Fortunately, the bishops and others seem highly intentional about recovering "conferencing" in its Wesleyan meaning. Will their exhortations to "conference together" really transform Methodist gatherings without also our/their making changes in the scale, site, composition, character and duties of meetings? What will suffice to make conferences again gracious? Those calling for holy conferencing need, perhaps, to ask more probing questions about the size, setting, and purposes of the gathering that would make conferences "holy."

Such queries point to a **second** affirmation that can be made about connectionalism and discerned in the "spirited" character of the Women's Congress. Connection and connectionalism have had, at their best, a pneumatological character. Methodist connectionalism, especially Methodist conferences, have lived in and off the spirit. That experientialism, that confidence in being led by the Spirit, has given Methodists the confidence to go with the Spirit, to experiment, to try new things, to change. In consequence, connectionalism has been *malleable, evolving, elastic, vulnerable.* Or, to relate this characteristic to one of the other classic marks of Methodism, connectionalism is and has been *forming and* *reforming.*[19] The Congress, though it exhibits characteristic Methodist patterns, is itself a new venture, founded and resourced by COSROW, a gathering to identify, excite, empower, mentor, and connect promising leaders. Nor is this the first connectional venture in sisterhood. There have been many, beginning with the homes that women, especially widows, kept for Asbury and his itinerants, continuing in the women's missionary societies, taking political form in Frances Willard's WCTU and institutionalizing itself in the deaconess and settlement houses.[20]

Connectional innovations have occurred periodically throughout Methodist history. Elsewhere I have identified a number of such innovations as successive stages and styles of connectionalism—communities of speech, camp meetinglike events, voluntary societies, the press, corporate program boards, professional associations, structures of accountability. In the several periods of its history, American Methodists found one of these particularly apt as a way of connecting to undertake their mission. So, in one epoch, the preaching event held the church together, in another a more organized camp meeting revivalism, in the next the network of Bible and Sunday schools societies, in another the energetic editors of the *Advocates,* in the late nineteenth and much of the twentieth century the boards and agencies, and in the late twentieth perhaps networks of professional gatherings and accountability structures. The point is, connectionalism changed. William Everett and Thomas Frank propose a similar but simpler scheme. They discern three models or theories of order in Methodism—public assembly, federalism, and corporatism.[21] Both their study and mine note that the several styles or models persist and therefore coexist, greatly complicating or enriching (depending on one's perspective) connectional life, fabric, and process.

These studies and others, then, distinguish the corporate or board and agency form of connectionalism, the most businesslike or machinelike style, as but one of several. And, impressions to the contrary, they show that corporate form or style is not just a reality that hovers over the congregation but is equally characteristic of local Methodism. The "local church" can be as "deformed" as the bureaucracies from which it often wishes to extricate itself financially and programmatically.[22] The local church can also be reformed and reform itself. In so doing, congregations participate in the transformation of the whole.

The potential power that local Methodism possesses to shape and reshape itself and its connection to the whole, and therefore to reshape the connection and connectionalism deserves notice. Transformation can come from below as well as by tinkering with denominational structures from above. Local experimentation, potentially productive of significant change, lies below the screen of most analyses of denominational structure and organization. And correlatively, congregational studies that have blossomed as a new significant area of research and publication tended to ignore structures above the local level. Quite promising, therefore, is the study by Penny Becker, which discerns four patterns of congregational ordering—house of worship, family, community, and leader styles—each with its distinctive set of strategies for dealing with the rest of the denomination. The first two, the familial and house of worship congregational styles, orient their members inward and not toward social engagement with the world or toward significant interaction with the denomination above the local level. The latter two patterns, on the other hand, either on an interest group basis or through the activities of its leadership, participate more actively with the connection and on connectional agendas.[23]

Becker's styles and strategies should be familiar. Less so will be the distinctive role each plays in negotiating connections with other denominational sectors and layers. Other initiatives which create new connectional fabric function from within congregations, also possess strong connectional dimensions, or perhaps one should say, potential. Several renewal ventures, for instance, connect United Methodists powerfully on the local level, among them Disciple, Emmaus Walk, Covenant Discipleship, and Volunteers in Mission. Their strong purposive or missional character creates strong bonds within and renews congregations. The connectional agencies, effective in the promotion of these and other programs, keep themselves in the background. The agencies have found ways of letting common enterprise, rather than structure, connect. A variety of other local and trans-local missional programs also exhibit potentially interesting connective patterns, typically featuring purpose rather than organizational structure. These might be seen as experiments in recreating connection from below, with inducement or provision from above.

New patterns of connectionalism could function with the connective realities of Western society—electronic culture, the computer and Internet, the various media, and other definers of our global society and economy. Such shifts would be dramatic for Methodism, argues Thomas Boomershine, since the movement has been defined by and was indeed structured for a print connectionalism. Highly successful in its use of hymnbooks, Sunday school materials, books, and *Advocates*, it has not as fully exploited the potential of electronic connectionalism and lacks a coherent electronic strategy.[24] Even with regard to television and the press, hardly new media, United Methodism has made fits and starts, lacks anything like a truly national strategy, does little to equip bishops and other leaders in media relations, fails to present itself in a compelling and coherent way on metropolitan and regional levels, and seems unable to project itself and its mission in an arena in which much of North America, particularly young America, shops for identity, values, and involvements.[25]

Connectionalism's malleability can be seen as well on the transnational and ecumenical level. United Methodism takes great pride of late in being a global church, by which it usually makes reference to those constitutive parts of the church in Africa, the Pacific, Asia, and Europe. United Methodism enjoys other forms of global connectionalism, as we will note more fully in chapter 4: through pan-Methodism, the World Methodist Council, the Churches Uniting in Christ (CUIC, formerly COCU), world, national, state, and local councils of churches, and bilateral dialogues. A full-orbed connectionalism and truly Wesleyan ecclesiology will claim various models of connectionalism (global or regional, confessional or interconfessional, denominational or pan-Wesleyan) and will invite United Methodism into a globalism expressive of its ecumenical witness and larger heritage.[26] Such new styles might, indeed probably would, differ from what we know now. But change has come regularly to Methodism's connections. Connectionalism is, then, *malleable, evolving, elastic, vulnerable—or forming and reforming*.

The expectation that connectionalism can be changed, even radically changed, and the perception that connectionalism—because of, despite, notwithstanding its reliance on the Spirit—has to do with nuts and bolts, with machinery, points to yet a **third** aspect of connectionalism. It is and has been a *tactical stratagem*, one taken to be providential. It works. It has worked. Perhaps the most hoary commonplace about nineteenth-century Methodist expansion, repeated by almost every interpreter, Methodist or non, was that Methodism succeeded because its tactics and mechanisms worked. It worked because of its itinerancy, the circuit riders, the connectional system, the conference structure, the appointive authority, camp meetings.[27] And all this they proclaimed "providential." Methodists can, then, be forgiven for thinking about connectionalism in functional terms because connectionalism has always had a functional quality. Its working has been important. Doubtless COSROW chose to convene a Women's Congress confident that such a gathering would indeed "call forth women leaders."

Extension ministries, as one of our essays shows, arose because they served unmet connectional needs. They had a tactical and strategic value. The church allowed them to evolve knowing them to be important (an earlier day would have pronounced them "providential"). The church did not figure how and still has not figured how to mesh some of the extension ministries into the existing connectional system. Indeed, in recent years a common presumption has been that only the parish counted as a scene for ministry. Clergy bemoan an individual as leaving the ministry when he or she relinquishes a local church appointment in favor of chaplaincy, a conference staff position, a post with a general agency, or a seminary professorship. Such marginalization of ministries intended to serve the connection as a whole constitutes a profound irony.[28] Happily, the term "extension" now applies to such connectional roles, replacing the unfortunate phrase "appointments beyond the local church," which canonized a congregational, very un-Wesleyan conception of ministry.

Strange as it may seem, another feature of Methodism (as of Protestantism generally) sometimes thought to be anti-connectional or divisive, namely the caucus, can as well be recognized for the way in which it connects individuals and groups from across the church around a common issue, cause, identity, role, or mission. These various late-twentieth-century ventures exhibit a range of connective strategies— grant-making, regulation, franchising, consulting, credentialing. Such organizations do distinguish and divide United Methodists into interest, caucus, or affinity groups—often now with a Web page and links to kindred bodies. They also connect the like-minded and can be every bit as joyful and sorrowful as the Women's Congress.[29] They divide, but they also connect. As my former colleague, Kenneth Rowe indicates, caucuses, campaigns, parties, and reform impulses have recurred through Methodist history; one day's prophetic, critical, adversarial body becomes the next day's denominational mandate or even a new denomination. Caucuses appear because they work and they work because they confront, challenge, and inspire a connection that itself prizes what works.[30]

A **fourth** aspect of connectionalism also has to do with how the parts relate to the whole, with stewardship, with the sharing of obligations and gifts. It might be termed an *ethic of equity and proportionality*. The currencies of stewardship vary. In the above vignette, the principle is represented in the efforts made to "share personal and spiritual stories through writing, singing, chanting, dancing, praying," through "hands-on mission work," through the emphasis on inclusivity, and through the provision for translators and signing. In these several ways, the Congress gathered from all participants, put energies into common endeavor, recognized the diversity of gifts, and found channels to resource the whole. These claims on the participants seem to have been joyfully accepted.

Less joy greets another common form of this ethic of equity and proportionality, namely apportionments. Indeed, to apportionments the language of crisis rather than joy would be more typically applied. And rather than binding together, apportionments may both reveal and stimulate strains and fissures in the connection and within a local church.[31] "Taxes" some call them, and a few tax-payer revolts have occurred with clear intent to send a message to the connection.

Notwithstanding some negative imaging, apportionments too have been among the ways to gather from all participants, put energies into common endeavor, recognize the diversity of gifts, and find channels to resource the whole. Apportionments constitute a kind of collective stewardship. However, apportionments constitute but one of many styles, currencies, and modes of proportionate connecting, as the activities of the Women's Congress and the imperatives Methodists have heard from Wesley suggest—sing our hymns, read our books, hold our doctrines, follow our discipline, share our mission, accept our appointments. Our currencies do abound. Further, apportionments constitute but one of many ways to achieve the financial dimension of such connecting. With Web sites, visual representations of missional objectives, electronic bidding, computerized budgeting, and the like, one can imagine a form of designated or elective giving as underwriting all that the denomination currently supports with apportionments. However undertaken, church finance is key to connectional style, mechanisms, self-understanding, and health.[32] Simple money raising is not the only object. How we join—financially, personally, purposively, spiritually—in common endeavor is what matters.[33] Our stewardship does indeed cover various currencies. And it is worth recalling that the office of steward was once one of the two key offices of local Methodism. The other was class leader. The latter stewarded things spiritual. The former stewarded things temporal.

The latter points suggest yet a **fifth** affirmation about connectionalism: It rests upon *covenantal commitment*. That covenant took transformative expression in the early class meetings. No less powerful covenants animated the women's missionary organization. Covenants undergirded our social witness, our social holiness. Covenants reverberate weekly in our sanctuaries as old members reaffirm their own vows in welcoming the new. Covenants undergird annual conferences. They find re-expression in Covenant Discipleship, Disciple, the Academy of Spiritual Formation, Emmaus Walk, Volunteers in Mission, and a variety of other renewal impulses that knit individuals into common endeavor locally and globally.[34] Conceivably, some form of covenanting has come or might come out of the Women's Congress. Clearly, the elements constitutive of covenanting are there.

Nowhere, perhaps, does the covenantal commitment take more self-conscious form than in the Council of Bishops (increasingly in cabinets and, in theory, in the new orders of elder and deacon). That dimension to the Council seems to be recent development. To be sure, the Council and its predecessor episcopal bodies have long had strong familial and conferencelike quality, the bonds of a shared role and common obligations, unique fraternal authority that sets the bishops off from other clergy, regular extended gatherings that permitted a growing together, deep emotional connections, sometimes of affection, sometimes of opposition. However, until recently this "fraternity" functioned with a strong, unwritten seniority system and restrictive code.[35]

Those aristocratic or patriarchal patterns have been challenged by a variety of developments, including the Council's diversity, the election of "rebellious cohorts," and cultural currents of collegiality. Particularly important have been the Council's efforts to function corporately in guiding the denomination and its intentionality about an inner life that would facilitate that guidance. The Council now divides into covenant discipleship groups and spends significant portions of meetings in these intimate gatherings. The bishops have put themselves under common spiritual disciplines. They have embraced missional and outreach projects together. They pray for one another. They labor to make their witness a united one and have restructured along missional or purposive lines. They use their sessions for edification as well as planning and ordering the life of the church. The familial style continues, but it has a more egalitarian than aristocratic feel. Covenants have supplanted "old-boy" networks.[36]

The Council, in its inner life as well as in the many duties of its members, exhibits a **sixth** element of connectionalism, its *missional principle*.[37] So also did the Women's Congress. The overall purpose of the Congress was missional, to empower women to play missional roles within the denomination. The event itself featured missional acts in Atlanta—in schools, a homeless shelter, safe-havens for battered women, AIDS ministries. And the design of the Congress was to put these "journey-takers" on the longer road of God's people. The entire affair had a directional character.

So has connectionalism been from the beginning, as Bishops Coke and Asbury made clear in insisting on the missional and connectional principle inherent in itinerancy:

How could an itinerant ministry be preserved through this extensive continent, if the yearly conferences were to station the preachers? They
would, of course, be taken up with the sole consideration of the spiritual
and temporal interests of that part of the connection, the direction of
which was entrusted to them. The necessary consequence of this mode of
proceeding would probably, in less than an age, be the division of the
body and the independence of each yearly conference. The conferences
would be more and more estranged from each other for want of a mutual
exchange of preachers: and that grand spring, the union of the body at
large, by which, under divine grace, the work is more and more extended
through this vast country, would be gradually weakened, till at last it
might be entirely destroyed. The connection would no more be enabled to
send missionaries to the western states and territories, in proportion
to their rapid population. The grand circulation of ministers would be at
an end, and a mortal stab given to the itinerant plan. The surplus of
preachers in one conference could not be drawn out to supply the defi-
ciencies of others, through declensions, locations, deaths, &c. and the
revivals in one part of the continent could not be rendered beneficial to the
others. Our grand plan, in all its parts, leads to an itinerant ministry. Our
bishops are travelling bishops. All the different orders which compose our
conferences are employed in the travelling line; and our local preachers
are, in some degree, travelling preachers. Everything is kept moving as far
as possible; and we will be bold to say, that, next to the grace of God, there
is nothing like this for keeping the whole body alive from the centre to the
circumference, and for the continual extension of that circumference on
every hand.[38]

So the connection, notes Thomas Frank, was missionally constituted,
built not from individual congregations, but around preaching, preaching points, and the preacher.[39] "Connectionalism is the covenantal association of preachers," indicates Richard Heitzenrater, "committed to
a united mission to spread scriptural holiness (and to abide by the doc-
trine/discipline of the organization designed to implement that mission)
under the direction of John Wesley and the conference." Connectionalism, he continues, "provided a centralized and united framework for
developing and effecting a common mission."[40]

To term connectionalism as missional is to recognize that in its very
structure, in its operations, in its daily life, Methodism was and is
evangelistic and reforming.[41] Its offices, as we see in another chapter,
functioned evangelistically. And the one most dramatically so was the
presiding eldership, now district superintendency. It served as the chief
missional, evangelistic, and strategic office of our church, a role that it
could, to advantage, reclaim.[42]

The American movement embraced and extended Methodism's missional direction, subtly revising the answer to Wesley's purpose query: "What may we reasonably believe to be God's Design in raising up the Preachers called *Methodists*?" to read: "To reform the Continent, and to spread scriptural Holiness over these Lands."[43] Gradually Methodism lived into that purpose, joining other evangelical Protestant denominations in the Protestant establishment, a shared missional endeavor at Christianizing American society and the world. The Methodist connections (MEC, UB, EA, AME, AMEZ, MP, MECS, etc.) served that purpose well. Even today, as Dennis Campbell indicates, Methodists continue to labor on behalf of a "residual establishment."[44]

The shape, features, structure, and decision making within Methodist connections altered as new missional challenges and opportunities occurred. By the shifts in missional purposes, as we noted above and elsewhere, can the stages of Methodist connectionalism be charted and described.[45] Moreover, each of the stages is derived from missional initiatives, sometimes undertaken by those outside the centers of power but often finding or inventing new ways to connect and claim the interest, involvement, and support of the church as a whole. So discovers Sarah Sloan Kreutziger with regard to deaconesses and the religious settlement movement in the early part of the twentieth century. These prophetic ventures took advantage of existing communication networks, especially among Methodist women; drew on the church's moral capital to further the cause of social reform; and made sisterhood connectional.[46] The men involved in urban ministry also connected nationally, cooperated ecumenically, drew laity into problem solving, trained seminarians, held up urban problems for the church as a whole, claimed connectional attention, and thereby gave the church a national urban strategy.[47]

Strategy has been ingredient in connectionalism from the start, though often implicit and only grasped after the fact, as it apparently was with John Wesley's creation of classes and conferences, indeed, the entire organizational grammar.[48] To speak with regard to his innovations or many that have followed, therefore, of a strategy or vision or ecclesial vision is to stretch, even abuse, a metaphor. Our **seventh** point, that connectionalism conveys or bears an *ecclesial vision*, requires some explanation. Vision suggests a looking ahead, a foreseeing, an anticipation of directions, whereas Methodists seem to embrace a mission, intuiting its rightness or appropriateness, and then discover meaning by looking back at, reflecting on, analyzing the mission. Ecclesial vision, then, may be the wrong metaphor (ecclesial praxis might be more apt) but since we have used it once we will do so again but with the just mentioned qualification. The design or end or purpose of mission has not always been first or foremost in Methodist minds, but in their collective commitment Methodists have discovered what it means to be the church. Connectionalism offers an ecclesial vision or ecclesial praxis, a Methodist way of being church.[49]

How then does something like hindsight become vision? How is it that Methodists act first and then explain? The theological premises that undergird this behavior derive from pneumatology and Christian experience. Methodists have trusted the Spirit and their individual/corporate spiritual experiences to guide them organizationally. Or at least they have looked on what they have just done and built and pronounced it providentially and spiritually given. And once the providential awareness dawns, once the presence of Spirit in organization is grasped, Methodists then celebrate, use, champion what connects. So nineteenth-century Methodists could celebrate the church's machinelike character because they experienced the Spirit in it and through what it did. And so those gathered at the Women's Congress evidence confidence that their gathering was Spirit-driven. "I saw the movement of the Holy Spirit in this place," one participant proclaimed. And the group behaved as though Spirit-driven, cheered by the anthem, "And I'm Going on Anyhow," understanding themselves as on a journey or a spiritual journey, viewing the gathering as journey takers.

Such "conferencing," we have suggested, most fully expresses the ecclesial vision, the church character of connectionalism. Wesley spoke of Christian conference as one of the five instituted means of grace (along with praying, searching the Scriptures, receiving the Lord's Supper, and fasting).[50] He meant by that the deep, probing engagement of persons in sustained conversation about one another's spiritual estate; about how the chains of sin might be loosed; about the effort needed to respond to grace; about the direction in which to move. Conferencing had indeed to do with spiritual journeys in which individuals moved with a group, were aided by a group, existed in the context of a group. Christian perfection spelled out the individual *telos*. Zion, a term American Methodists used for their connection, spelled out the corporate *telos*. Connectionalism, especially as conferencing, has constituted a way of being "church." In that sense, then, ecclesial vision is apt.

Not all conferencing leads to Zion, and not all conversation leads to perfection. Methodists segregated their gatherings early and, as late as the mid-twentieth century, built racist scandal into the national structure of the denomination (in the all black Central Jurisdiction and all white overlapping southern jurisdictions). Jurisdictions may be connective structures that have outlived their dubious usefulness. The Council of Bishops we have celebrated for its connectional and conferencing character. But not all actual practices around and of bishops can be so celebrated. Episcopal elections, though dramatizations of connectionalism, sometimes bring out sordid, even base behavior and dimensions of corporate life.[51]

For connectionalism to carry United Methodism's best sense of being church, for it to be an ecclesial vision worth having, it does need to be shaped by the Spirit within and without. It must orient the church toward the world in spiritual fashion. That means, as we have already indicated, bearing the church into mission. Connectionalism also means discerning the church's appropriate boundaries and treating the neighbor beyond those boundaries appropriately. Should United Methodism understand and structure its connections to other Christian churches confessionally or interconfessionally, and at what level—globally, nationally, regionally, locally?[52] To this issue we return in chapter 4.

As United Methodism thinks through its alternatives for the future, as it faces its alternative futures, it will doubtless reflect first on structure. Cynics compare this to shuffling chairs on the *Titanic*. However, if the church has indeed vested its sense of itself, its ecclesial vision, its mission in connectional program, structure, and fabric, where else should it begin? And does not the church's most encompassing sense of its mission, namely its responsibilities and prospects in American society, come to focus in what it will attempt through its programs and structures?[53] Similarly, the local mission of Methodism requires clarity about outreach structures and programs. Methodism's relation to the wider community, its public policy, involves connectionalism as well as its Social Principles.[54]

Our **eighth** and final affirmation about connectionalism is that it is a *Wesleyan precept,* a claim about heritage, identity, location, parentage. This dimension of connectionalism the Women's Congress exhibited in its attention to foremothers, in the official leadership present, in the Methodist practices used, in the priority on storytelling. In these informal narrative ways, if not by more explicit declaration, the Congress claimed the Wesleyan mantle.

Fidelity in the Wesleyan tradition has had, we suggest, just such a narrative character. Individually and collectively Methodists have told their faith story, and in so doing they are connecting themselves with one another and connecting themselves with Wesley and connecting themselves with the longer Christian witness. The love feast featured such witnessing, early conferences featured such witnessing, and Methodist serials (papers and magazines) featured such witnessing. Such narratives had a definite shape. They traced the tortuous road from sin to salvation. They echoed the refrains of Charles Wesley. They enacted an Arminian theology. And by language, metaphor, typology, and story they brought Scripture into life.

Confessional and explicitly doctrinal Methodists have not always been. However, adherence to Wesley, to his connectional mandates, to his practices, to his authority, to his teaching has been constitutive of American Methodism from the beginning. The first *Minutes* so founded the movement:

> The following queries were proposed to every preacher:
>
> 1. Ought not the authority of Mr. Wesley and that conference, to extend to the preachers and people in America, as well as in Great-Britain and Ireland?
> *Answ.* Yes.
>
> 2. Ought not the doctrine and discipline of the Methodists, as contained in the minutes, to be the sole rule of our conduct who labour in connection with Mr. Wesley in America?
> *Answ.* Yes.
>
> 3. If so, does it not follow that if any preachers deviate from the minutes, we can have no fellowship with them till they change their conduct?
> *Answ.* Yes.[55]

Wesleyan identity has been precious, so precious that in disputes, reforms, and schisms each party has claimed the Wesleyan mantle. So the early black Methodist denominations, the Methodist Protestants, the Wesleyans, and the Free Methodists defined themselves as the true loyalists to the heritage, identity, message, and discipline.[56] So Methodism has forged its intellectual life grounding invention and creativity in Wesley's practice if not always his proclamation.[57] So reformers and builders have claimed Wesleyan precedent.[58] So, in one way or another, Methodists name themselves so as to trumpet their connection to Mr. Wesley. They narrate their adherence.

Implications: Connection and Church

In these several ways, then, Methodists have "marked" their life together, their connectedness, their shared mission. They have practiced connectionalism. Their practice has been nuanced, complex, thematically rich. Only infrequently have Methodists teased out these meanings, as we have sought to do here. The effort proves worthwhile. For instance,

Judith Smith conducted a number of interviews with bishops, and she nicely captures the complexity and intricacies of connection as manifested in episcopal expectations, leadership, and roles: Connection is visionary, communal, rooted in the tradition(s), widely embraced, holistic, creative, motivating, collegial, spiritual, oriented to life experiences, functional, relational, authentic, charismatic.[59] Here and there one can find other dramatizations or summations of United Methodism's connectional self-understanding. Ironically a particularly well-developed exegesis of connectionalism could, for a period, be found exactly where one would want it. The *Disciplines* for 1988 and 1992 carried an eloquent section entitled "The Journey of a Connectional People." It spoke of connection as shared vision, memory, community, discipline, leadership, mobilization, and linkage. The several-page treatment developed each motif theologically and historically.[60]

With the removal of that section, the denomination has left the ecclesial meaning of connection rather more implicit or diffused through the *Discipline.*[61] The same might be said of United Methodism's theology of church as a whole. In the *Discipline,* the church certainly exhibits its ecclesiological creedal statements, lays out its doctrinal self-understanding eloquently, situates Methodist theology in relation to the longer Christian heritage, says much about ministry, and devotes a huge section to the local church. Mission, ministry, and structure receive their due. A formal ecclesiology, a well-developed doctrine of the church, does not seem to hold all the church references together. One can scarcely say that the *Discipline* neglects to say anything about the church. It says much. However, "church" functions for Methodists adjectivally rather than substantively. The index to the Discipline tells the tale. Over two pages of references detail Methodist adjectival use of "church":

church conference	church school publications
church council	church school
church founding date	church school superintendent
church historian	church secretaries
church local conference	church-state separation
church location and building	churchwide appeal
church membership	churchwide offerings
[longest list of entries]	church women united
church name outside U.S.A.	church and community work
church property	church and society
church-related institutions	

One little entry on "Church, the" points to a few stray disciplinary paragraphs. Hardly the way more creedal churches would present their ecclesiology.

Even today, then, Methodists prove better at being church than explaining their practice doctrinally. There is, however, in the life of the church, in its heritage, and even spread throughout the *Discipline,* a rich sense of connectionalism waiting to be teased into a formal ecclesiology. The practice has not been neglected.

Understanding Connection Scripturally

Quite a number of passages might be cited as important in understanding Wesleyan or Methodist conceptions of connection, particularly passages out of the Synoptic Gospels. Other texts bear note, for instance, John 15 (especially 15:7-17) and the latter chapters of 1 Corinthians (especially 12:4–13:13). The vine image in John and the body imagery in Paul might have proved, over the long haul, more theologically suggestive and ecclesially helpful than the machine metaphors that Methodism introduced early on and has sustained ever since. Both images orient us to the church as connected and connectional.

Either image would have kept Methodists pneumatologically and christologically conscious and self-conscious. They would have been and would be less tempted to think only practically and strategically about things connectional. Instead, they would have known that the connection as vine lives as part of the true vine, as a branch alive only in its connection to the vine, kept alive in the love shared within the Holy Trinity and suffused through the whole plant. They would have known that as members of the Body of Christ, they work together, constantly remembering their head, indeed kept vibrant and connected by his presence in their midst and in their hearts, bearing in some degree the eucharistic joy conveyed to them regularly. Such theological assessments of connectionalism, if not prominent in our heritage, can nevertheless be introduced today.

Having taken note of the ecclesial promise for Methodism in such Johannine and Pauline images, I would suggest that American Methodists have lived more out of the Synoptics and Pastorals. They have concerned themselves in the first instance with discipleship and with making disciples, and they have not worried themselves as much over the nature of the unity they experienced in the Spirit and with Christ. They have been itinerant, on the road with Jesus. They have sat down with him in the fellowship meal. They have sought to do what Jesus would have them do.

Their ecclesiology, largely implicit, took its cues from the Synoptics, from being on the road and especially at table with Jesus. They dramatized "church" in the love feast and in the Lord's Supper. Later they animated "church" in the Sunday school movement in which Methodists took lead, honeycombing the church with the small cells in which growth in the Spirit could occur. And in the present, the ecclesial impulse, the connectional reality expresses itself in the Disciple Bible Study movement, in Covenant Discipleship, in Emmaus Walk, in Volunteers in Mission, in Alpha, and in various similar communal and communitarian ventures (for instance, the *Women's Congress*).

In the stories of Jesus on the road and at table, Methodists have found images for their collective life, an ecclesiology practiced but not adequately theologized. It was, however, an ecclesiology they could sing:

> Joined in one spirit to our Head,
> Where he appoints we go;
> And still in Jesu's footsteps tread,
> And show his praise below.

Conclusion

Methodists have looked back on the camp meeting as one of their distinctive institutions. Such it was. To succeed, the camp meeting took a tremendous amount of planning, effort, structure, organization, resources, talent, leadership. When so ordered, the camp meeting made festival and feast possible. The camp meeting attested the effectiveness of Methodist machinery and the vibrancy of the Methodist spirit. The machine made the life possible. But, and Methodists have long forgotten this, the machine was the life and the life was the machine. Methodists held so many camp meetings because they appointed one of their warm-weather quarterly meetings (their charge conference) in the camp. The camp meeting was not something extra or instrumental, not just a staging ground for revival. It was Methodism organized, missional, evangelistic, eucharistic, Spirit-filled. It looked a lot like the Women's Congress.

While the camp meeting geared Methodist machinery for quarterly conference festival, it also opened itself to all Christians and especially the unsaved. The camp meeting oriented the Methodist connection toward the world. Though few would have grasped it at the time and we have certainly lost sight of it today, the connectionalism expressed in the camp meeting—its lovefeastlike, festival, affectionate, narrative pattern—exhibited both the quality of the unity within Methodism and the reality of a unity more broadly shared within the Christian family, indeed within the whole family of God.

At its best, Methodist connectionalism pointed and points beyond institutional and confessional lines to the unity shared in Christ, a point that John Wesley made variously and that radiates triumphantly through Charles Wesley's hymn. We return to this theme in the chapter on catholicity. A community genuinely bound together in the love of Christ knows no boundaries imposed out of human frailties.

CHAPTER TWO

Itinerant

1 JESUS, thy servants bless,[1]
Who, sent by thee, proclaim
The peace, and joy, and righteousness
Experienced in thy name:
The kingdom of our God,
Which thy great Spirit imparts,
The power of thy victorious blood,
Which reigns in faithful hearts.

2 Their souls with faith supply,
With life and liberty;
And then they preach and testify
The things concerning thee:
And live for this alone,
Thy grace to minister,
And all thou hast for sinners done
In life and death declare.

Itinerancy, this Methodist pattern of ministry?[2] What is it? What does the word mean? Why have Methodists employed it, emphasized it, insisted on it, understood both bishop and the elder thereby? Does either really still itinerate? Does itinerancy really persist? Should it? Or is it broken, compromised, dead? If so, should we care? Should we mourn?

Does itinerancy have essentially to do with movement, with travel, with change? And does it primarily refer to the circuit system, as inaugurated by John Wesley, and as institutionalized in frontier North America? Does it pertain, historically and accurately, to travel around the circuit and then traveling from one circuit to one's appointment on the next? Do we use it, by extension and perhaps too facilely, for location and deployment and for relocation and redeployment?

Does it now mean being moved (if one is an elder or in the family thereof)? Or losing one's much beloved minister (if one is a member)? In the former's perspective, especially that of the ministerial spouse, is it about being under appointment; going to a place in ministry; settling down and making friends; setting up oneself in business, a profession, various community roles; connecting with all the necessary services, doctors and dentists, day care, hairdressers and barbers; learning the school system; finding or establishing the networks that get the kids picked up from day care or to soccer after school; finding a vet for the cat and dog; in short, settling into community, into congregational leadership roles, into good family order, into a disciplined life? Then the phone rings and one hears, "This is District Superintendent (D.S.) Simon Legree. How are you? Is your spouse available?" And without listening in, the family knows that they will be leaving friends, jobs, all the networks and systems, everything put into order over months and even years.

And all those party to the arrangement—clergy, clergy family, congregation, colleague ministers in other denominations, community leaders—ask "Why?" Why change this effective ministry? Why now? Why do Methodists mess up a working congregational system, why upset family connections and involvements, why put relationships in turmoil in this way? Why? Why does Methodist leadership (D.S. and Bishop) seemingly ignore a ministry that seems to be highly successful? Why does it show such apparent disrespect for parish and family order? Why does it insist on sending minister and family into a wholly new, often distant setting? Why itinerancy?

And why since 1808, and the General Conference of that year, has the Methodist Episcopal Church and successor denominations protected an itinerant general superintendency as Methodism's style of episcopacy? The Restrictive Rules stipulated that

> The general conference shall have full powers to make rules and regulations for our church, under the following limitations and restrictions, viz.

> 3. They shall not change or alter any part of rule of our government, so as to do away Episcopacy or destroy the plan of our itinerant general superintendency.

Why itinerancy? Because it is the Methodist pattern? Because Mr. Wesley embraced and institutionalized it? Because Francis Asbury imposed it by precept, command, and example? Because we have always done it that way? Because it functions as well as alternative systems? Because it worked/works? Because it effectively deploys ministers, and it guarantees every pastor a church and every church a minister?

What constitutes itinerancy—the traveling, the appointment, the self-understanding, the relation to conference, the insurance system, the tenure, the covenant, the commitment to accept an appointment, the promise that one will be extended?

Is that it: the denominational way? inertia? precedent? mechanics? pragmatism? Is itinerancy just an organizational style? Is it merely a human relations system? Is it essentially management?

Or might itinerancy have less to do with mechanics than with theology? Might there be implicit in itinerancy an understanding of the gospel, of church, and of the ministry? Might itinerancy—and the next move, and the next one after that—have to do fundamentally with how Methodists understand God to work in the world? Might itinerancy be predicated on a conception of the Kingdom and of the church captured in the Wesley verse that begins: "JESUS, thy servants bless, Who, sent by thee . . ." "Who, sent by thee!"

A Mirror on Itinerancy?

So how do we as Methodists think about itinerancy? Don't we revert to the figure of Francis Asbury or to his times? Don't we think that itinerancy has to do essentially with moves and movement? with travel? with riding?

The term *itinerant* conjures up the image on United Methodist clergy's *Daily Suggester,* that of the lonely rider. The lonely rider, the solitary horseman, the man against the elements—virtually a trademark of Methodist ministry—unfortunately captures only a small part of what itinerancy was intrinsically meant to be, actually was, and should be. If we take Asbury's day to mirror itinerancy, let us look more deeply into that glass. We could do so with Asbury. As "itinerant general superintendent" par excellence he did indeed model the itinerant pattern.[3] A less exceptional and more typical representation can be drawn from William Colbert (1764–1835). A native of Maryland, drawn into the itinerancy in 1790, ordained elder in 1792, appointed to circuits over much of the east (Maryland, Delaware, New Jersey, Pennsylvania, New York), several times a presiding elder, stalwart opponent of slavery, Colbert proved to be a man unusually careful, consistent, and persistent in his journaling. Colbert recorded many days that conform to our image of the lonely rider. He also routinely recalled very different days of travel, as these for his 1796–97 appointment to the Bristol circuit illustrate. Note the pronouns in the following vignette. (Unfinished sentences, by the way, indicate material I omitted, leaving pronouns and verbs to which I would call especial attention.)

Vignette

Saturday [Sept.] 2 [1797] We held a Quarterly meeting at our friend Konkles in Milton . . . at night we had a prayer meeting at our friend Gibbs's.

Sunday 3 We have had a good Love feast this morning. Brother Jefferson preached . . . he brought forward some very strong argument against the Calvinistic System. I preached after him, administered the sacrament and Baptized some children. . . .

Monday 4 We spent . . .

. . .

Wednesday 6 heard Hamilton Jefferson preach . . . I gave an exhortation after him.

Thursday 7 We rode . . .

Friday 8 I preached. . . . Brother Jefferson gave a lively exhortation after me.

Saturday 9 We held our last Quarterly meeting at George Wheelers . . .

Sunday 10 We have had a profitable Love feast this morning. Bro. Jefferson preached . . . I preached . . .

Tuesday 12 took our leave of the circuit . . .

[Entries for the following days indicate that he rode with Hamilton Jefferson]

Saturday 16 attended a Quarterly meeting at Henry Salsberys at Tonda . . .

[He continued riding with Hamilton Jefferson the next week]

Saturday 23 On my way to a Quarterly meeting at Gilbert Carpenters in Wyoming

   [An event with two sermons and exhortations in afternoon, two sermons and four exhortations in evening, each was undertaken by a different preacher]

Sunday 24 We had a profitable Love feast in Esq. Carpenters house, which was succeeded by three sermons. . . . The sacrament was then administered, and brother Wilson gave an exhortation and concluded the meeting . . .

. . .

Tuesday 26 Started from Wilksbarre for Philadelphia. A man by the name of Moody fell in with us, as he appeared to be a decent man we meant to use him with good manners, but we soon found he was a Deist. I was pestered with him for several miles before brother Jefferson was kind enough to take him off my hands . . .

Wednesday 27 This morning another man took off our Deist, and we were glad enough to get rid of him. . . .

Thursday 28 Hamilton Jefferson preached . . . I spoke after him . . . and brother Wilson concluded the meeting. . . .

Friday 29 We rode . . .

Saturday 30 We visited Bethlehem . . .

Sunday Oct. 1 H. Jefferson preached . . . bro. Wilson spoke after him, and I concluded the meeting.

. . .

Tuesday 3 At night H. Jefferson preached . . .

Wednesday 4 we rode . . .

Thursday 5 we rode . . .

Friday 6 rode . . .

Saturday 7 we rode . . .

Sunday 8 We rode into Wilmington and heard Ezekiel Cooper preach in the forenoon. . . . In the afternoon I rode to New Port, and preached . . . Michael Wilson gave an exhortation after me. In the evening Hamilton Jefferson preached . . . Anning Owen exhorted after him. . .

Monday 9 We fell in company with a large number of preachers on our way to Duck Creek where we are to hold our conference. . . . At night Jesse Lee preached, John McClaskey gave a warm exhortation . . .

Tuesday 10 Our conference began—Business went on but slow. Several were received. Richard Swain preached an animating discourse. . . .

Wednesday 11 Bishop Asbury preached . . . , Ezekiel Cooper and Richard Swain exhorted. All the preachers present passed their examination.

Thursday 12 a time of refreshing from the presence of the Lord while Jesse Lee was preaching . . .

Friday 13 Bishop Asbury preached . . . , John Lackey, and Joseph Jewell were ordained Deacons. Hamilton Jefferson and Anning Owen were ordained Elders.

Saturday 14 Spent part of the day in writing. At night Thomas Ware preached . . . McClaskey, Bunn and Sharp exhorted. . . .

Sunday 15 a Love feast was held this morning . . . At 10 oc Bishop Asbury preached . . . In the afternoon Ezekiel Cooper preached . . . and at night Jesse Lee . . . At this conference the charge of Chester and Strasburg Circuit was given to me. William P. Chandler travels with me.

Monday 16 Rode with Anning Owen . . .
Tuesday 17 We rode to Wilmington.
. . .
Friday 20 Met my Colleague Doctor Chandler . . .[4]

Commentary

Several aspects of this journal, of the pace and style of itinerancy, deserve remark. In Colbert's journaled experience a number of the key features of itinerancy come readily into view. Seven might be noted:

Itinerancy is communal.
Itinerancy is cooperative.
Itinerancy is missionary or evangelical.
Itinerancy is appointed/appointive/under authority.
Itinerancy is connectional.
Itinerancy is commissioned.
Itinerancy is a covenantal, a spiritual journey.

First, itinerancy is *communal.* Note the pronouns that recur throughout the passage.

Note the recurrent "we rode." Colbert spent a month and a half riding from his last quarterly conferences to annual conference. For much of that pilgrimage, he rode, not alone, as our image would have it, but with his ministerial comrade from an adjacent circuit. They

rode all day together,
jointly conducted services,
ate together,
bedded down at the same waystation,
converged with others at quarterly meetings and
eventually joined the great in-gathering of the traveling preachers
at annual conference.

Colbert itinerated. He rode but frequently not alone. He rode in company with colleagues and for an extended period. His riding with others on the way to conference took from early September to mid-October because of the distance he had to travel to conference. Itinerants closer to conference would not have left their appointments as early nor faced such a long ride. However, Colbert's pattern typified itinerant practice. The preachers would meet so as to ride together. Later when they could travel by rail, the preachers would congregate on the train for a comparable riding together, swapping tales, summing up the year, sharing wisdom, learning from one another.

Entirely typical, also, was the riding together around to quarterly meetings, to one's own of which there were of course four a year, and to those on neighboring circuits to be attended if at all possible. From the last batch of quarterly conferences, preachers readily formed a caravan to annual conference. So the itinerant might appropriately be imaged as on a corporate journey, a corporate journey that was punctuated by stints of travel on his own.[5] Itinerancy is communal or, in an earlier day, fraternal.

Second, *cooperative.* Methodism made its early appointments not as individuals, but as teams, two to a circuit—Colbert and Joseph Whitby to Bristol for the 1796–97 year, Colbert and Chandler to Chester and Strasburg for the 1797–98 year. The team approach had several purposes. One dimension of arrangement was pedagogical. Teaming made it possible to put a neophyte with a seasoned preacher. Such apprenticing and mentoring constituted the ministerial training and theological education of that day. The senior member modeled ministry; heard the junior's efforts at praying, exhorting, and preaching; offered encouragement, counsel, and correction; and then provided colleagues with an endorsement or criticism when the junior's name came up for review of character or admission.

The team members cared for one another. The riding together often forged very close, lifelong bonds, bonds captured in a term used to describe the arrangement, *yokefellows.* Letters exchanged between those who traveled together have the quality and tone of love letters. They convey powerful sentiments of intimacy, care, affirmation, respect. Family-like relations pertained, some father-to-son, others more brother-to-brother. The yokes of itinerancy represented shared mission, shared work, shared finances, shared flock, shared adversity, shared revival. Itinerancy is cooperative.

Third and perhaps most important, it is *missionary.* Itinerancy meant being sent, being sent to a circuit, being moved from one circuit that one now knew into one where one went as missionary.[6] Elsewhere in his journal, Colbert grumbled about being sent to northern areas. He much preferred placements in his own Philadelphia-Baltimore orbit. But being a traveling preacher meant being sent, going with the authority of a Methodist preacher, representing the connection, serving as missionary, carrying the Methodist version of the gospel. The connection itself was missionary because it hung together as a series of preaching appointments to which the itinerants individually and corporately assigned themselves.[7]

Itinerancy meant that preachers could be sent where, in the judgment of the bishop, they would serve best or were most needed. Then as now, those appointed were not always as confident as the bishops in the wisdom or strategic value of their appointment. But the theory was that the whole collective of preachers were being employed with the mission in mind.

Although deployed to a circuit as missionary, the preacher went knowing that he was not alone. One was sent to a particular circuit but as part of a team. The team traveled out as part of a caravan. And all went realizing that all were being sent out. Being sent had its lonely days but under a corporate imperative. The *Annual Minutes* registered that corporate imperative in specifying each and all's appointment.

Itinerancy was missionary, of course, in the sense that the appointment and the preaching were for revival. Conversion, revival, beginning the disciplined life toward holiness, forming classes to nurture and sustain the converts constituted the work of itinerancy. At the end of the appointive period, even just an appointive year, the preacher yearned to report a revival. Itinerancy is missionary or evangelical.

Fourth, itinerancy is *appointive*. Itinerancy involved honoring appointments. Bishops, beginning with Asbury, have put that expectation imperatively: "Never disappoint an appointment!" Asbury had more in mind than that annual appointment or change of appointment when he proclaimed and reiterated, "Never disappoint an appointment! Never disappoint an appointment!"

Itinerants lived with multiple appointments. Two appointments launched the itinerant's ministry: First the bishop appointed the itinerant to the circuit and second one's predecessor tentatively set individual preaching appointment (and handed over a plan as conference adjourned). Itinerancy thereafter involved continuously setting appointments for oneself and others—for one's yokefellow on the circuit, for local preachers, for one's presiding elder, for other preachers who would come to assist, and eventually for one's successor. Itinerancy honored mutual obligations.

Laboring under appointments required trust—trust in the one that appointed, trust that the right appointment would be given one, trust in what one's predecessor had done, had said, had set up, trust in one's yokefellow, trust in oneself, trust in the people with whom one worked. And all those acts of trust needed to be reciprocated. Appointment created a variety of mutual bonds and required assent to the authority that would sustain them. Itinerancy is appointive—under authority.

Fifth, itinerancy is *connectional.* Bishops Thomas Coke and Francis Asbury made it clear, in their annotations of the *Discipline,* that Wesley-like itinerancy, particularly their itinerancy and their appointment of preachers out of their circulation through the entirety of the Methodist work, connected and united the movement.

> Our *grand plan,* in all its parts, leads to an *itinerant* ministry. Our bishops are *travelling* bishops. All the different orders which compose our conferences are employed in the *travelling line;* and our local preachers are, *in some degree,* travelling preachers. Everything is kept moving as far as possible; and we will be bold to say, that, next to the grace of God, there is nothing *like this* for keeping the whole body alive from the centre to the circumference, and for the continual extension of that circumference on every hand.[8]

All these diverse traveling bonds—traveling together, serving in teams, traveling as one sent, traveling to appointments that others set—inhered in the covenant that made the connection.[9] The covenant bound individuals into a corporate brotherhood, into a shared mission, under a common Arminian gospel, with obligations to those sent as well as to one's peers. Conference itself embodied and reinforced those bonds. Cementing and symbolizing those bonds were the common rituals of admission, common patterns of probation, common adversities on the road, a *common salary,* much common time together, and a common table.

The preachers knew themselves to share one table and experienced that, quite literally, at conference. A family gathering, a meeting of separated brothers, a time of spiritual renewal, an occasion for resourcing, an opportunity to trade stories—conference combined elements of religious festival and family gathering with the business of assessing probationers, judging one's peers, legislating on common concerns, and reconciling finances. Colbert appreciated the festival/familial character and hardly bothered to note what business conference did. Who preached and who exhorted concerned him.[10] Itinerancy is connectional.

Sixth, itinerancy is *commissioned.* Itinerancy indeed meant being connected; having one's primary allegiance to church, gospel, Lord; taking on the identity of itinerancy; traveling on the Lord's commission. It had to do with mobility, travel, and a horse because of what these made possible. Itinerancy quite literally connected Methodism, but connected it for its purpose—preaching. The connection was, as Frank notes, built around preaching points.[11] Preaching the Word defined and characterized Methodist ministers. They bore that identity. They were preachers—

not parish ministers, not clergy, not priests. Preachers they called themselves, were called, were so denominated in the *Discipline.*

Commissioned and called to preach, the itinerants bore in their person a fundamentally different understanding of church than that which dominated Western Christendom. Communions with a state-church background—Anglican, Lutheran, Reformed, Roman Catholic—functioned with a parish ideal, a regional mapping of the landscape so as to provide one parish church for each community. Communions shaped by Puritanism or the free church ideal imagined a local gathering coalescing into a congregation. Either way, the local unit, the congregation, was theoretically stable and to it the minister would be called or would go. Methodists, well into the nineteenth century, lacked such stable local units. Originally Methodists held their membership in a class, the composition and leadership of which was in the preacher's hands. The basic local unit was the quarterly conference. And the preachers, both traveling and local, deployed themselves on a circuit, even in urban areas. Only very gradually did classes and societies stabilize their identity through a church building; only gradually did such stations receive appointments on their own, and Methodism begin to develop viable congregations. Even then, however, the appointment was to the charge, whether as a station or a circuit.

Initially, then, and in theory, Methodists stood the ecclesial sequence on its head. The prevailing norm was, first call a congregation into being, then call a pastor. For Methodists it was, first commission a preacher, and then send him to call the lost into communion. Instead of being called to a congregation, the preacher called the church into being. The church depended on the preacher's call rather than the other way around. Methodism operationalized this understanding, this theology of church and of ministry by lodging the ordination procedures and rituals in conference. The process began in quarterly conference, which heard the narrative of a call to preach; issued the license; assessed quarterly the character, gifts, and grace for ministry; and eventually recommended a candidate to annual conference. There, after a probationary period and similar assessment, the preacher would be ordained and given his commission. Itinerancy is commissioned.

Seventh, itinerancy is *covenantal, a spiritual journey.* Itinerancy necessitated several types of travel—travel in space, in time, around a circuit, to conference, to the new appointment, and to its various obligations—physical travel. Itinerancy necessitated travel in exploration of one's call, with a mentoring preacher, through the probationary process, into conference membership, through annual reviews of character, and toward holiness—spiritual travel. Physical and spiritual travel went together, involved the same movements, shared resting and renewal locales. A prominent feature of Colbert's journal, as of others, was several spiritual movements, several ways in which itinerancy involved spiritual journeying only hinted at in the above selection.

The spiritual journey of itinerancy first meant traveling upward, along the long road to perfection, the *via salutis*, the path to the Kingdom. The journals mark out this spiritual journey. They often start retrospectively, with the individual's early religious struggles, a recollection written after conversion and call, when already preaching and facing the inevitable doubts and feelings of inadequacy of early ministry. Within his longer Christian pilgrimage toward heaven, the itinerant now locates his current inner vocational turmoil. Then the journals take up his further travels in the faith as well as into ministry. They carry the writer and reader through a physical landscape that also landscapes the writer's personal journey along the way marked out by John Wesley. Daily entries remark on trials and tribulations on the road and also the struggles of the spiritual walk, on physical hardships and spiritual turmoil. Not infrequently, the itinerant needed a stop to bring the two travels into accord. He then retired to a woods or to a quiet room for solace, prayer, quiet.

Second, one traveled into ministry onwardly, in the way indicated above—by being taken on the road by another preacher who saw in the neophyte promise for ministry. Individuals who showed some signs of promise for the traveling ministry, as class leaders perhaps, would travel with the itinerant around the circuit as a way of beginning the long road of ministry. That riding into one's call often involved travel out of and back into one's former life, its family context and worldly inducements. The call to preach battled the allure of home, society, security. Not infrequently preachers represented the temptations to quit traveling as from Satan. Physical and imaginative travel back home contended with the spiritual disciplines undertaken on the road under the guidance of other preachers. Probationary riding spiritually needed the actual riding with one's yokefellow and other compatriots, needed the communal support of quarterly conference, needed the disciplines of the *Discipline,* needed the road out of the world. Being drawn out spiritually, itinerancy began as an invitation to travel to test out one's calling.

Third, itinerancy involved traveling inward—from distant quarterly conference to annual conference, the first of such trips being as one recommended on trial. Subsequent trips would be to have one's character assessed, to be examined for full connection, and then to play a role as a traveling preacher both in assessing others and being assessed. The journals record the itinerant's efforts to hold himself accountable to connectional expectations—of study, prayer, fasting. Itinerancy involved the annual travel into trial. And such inward journeys required use of the several means of grace, including the oft-noted retirement to the wood for prayer.

Fourth, itinerancy meant traveling outward from conference to circuit, a journey away from one's brothers in ministry, a journey with them as long as possible, and then into what was often a new and strange region. Such entry and experience of loneliness while one's yokefellow went elsewhere on the circuit has given us the image of the solitary rider. This road took the itinerant into his vocation, into the exercise of his calling.

And fifth, itinerancy involved traveling around one's circuit, a journey that often recapitulated the prior kinds of travel. The first weeks on a new circuit would be strange, challenging, threatening, call-questioning. The itinerant would not know the people or their spiritual estate, nor have their trust. Gradually the promise of the circuit would appear as persons along the stops would respond to the itinerant and his ministry, particularly his preaching. By the end of the conference year, the preacher would take tearful good-byes at the fourth quarterly conferences, feel painfully the separation from the people whose spiritual journeys he had become part of, and head back to annual conference to receive another appointment and begin the cycle again. And so, we can affirm that itinerancy is a covenantal, spiritual journey.

Itinerancy was, then, more than just a man and a horse. It constituted a complex metaphor for a multi-faceted ministry, a variety of journeys, and a corporate itinerancy—ministry carried on connectionally, as much with one's peers as apart from them. Itinerancy was communal, cooperative, missionary or evangelical, appointed/appointive/under authority, connectional, commissioned, covenantal, spiritual journeying.

Itinerancy: The Apostolic Pattern

If early American Methodists did not exegete itinerancy precisely in the above fashion, they championed it ferociously. They were clear that itinerancy occupied a very central place in the Methodist movement and would have recognized the above traits as so characterizing it, had they been named. They affirmed it, of course, as a Wesleyan mandate. More important, they affirmed itinerancy because they saw it as the biblical pattern, the apostolic pattern, the pattern of Christ's own ministry. Like Christ and like those he sent out, the itinerants were sent:

> JESUS, thy servants bless,
> Who, sent by thee, proclaim
> The peace, and joy, and righteousness
> Experienced in thy name:
> The kingdom of our God,
> Which thy great Spirit imparts,
> The power of thy victorious blood,
> Which reigns in faithful hearts.

Thomas Coke and Francis Asbury, who annotated the *Discipline* in 1798, made absolutely clear that itinerancy, their itinerancy as bishops and that of the preachers, reclaimed the primitive pattern of ministry. They cited the following scripture as "in support of the itinerant plan for the prop-agation of the gospel": Matthew 10:5-11; 22:8-10; 28:19; Mark 6:7-12; Luke 10:1-9; 14:23; Acts 8:4; 8:40; 16:36. They claimed that "Timothy and Titus were travelling bishops" and insisted that "every candid person, who is thoroughly acquainted with the New Testament, must allow, that what-ever excellencies other plans may have, *this* is the primitive and *apostolic plan*."[12] Methodists believed itinerancy was so essential to the apostolic plan that they identified, indeed, equated it with episcopacy. From the start, the *Discipline* insisted on what later would be formulated in the Restrictive Rules as "**itinerant general superintendency**," the Methodist "doctrine" of **episcopacy**:

> Q. If the *Superintendent* ceases from Travelling at large among the People, shall he still exercise his Office in any Degree?
>
> A. If he cease from Travelling without the Consent of the Conference, he shall not thereafter exercise any ministerial Function whatsoever in our Church.[13]

Coke and Asbury commented at length on the apostolic character of Methodist itinerancy in relation to bishop, presiding elder, and preacher. They insisted that it was scriptural *and* distinctive. In particular they knew that itinerant episcopacy differed radically from other forms.

> The bishops are obliged to travel, till the general conference pronounces them worn-out or superannuated: for that certainly is the meaning of the answer to the 6th question of this section. What a restriction! Where is the like in any other episcopal church? It would be a disgrace to our episcopacy,

to have bishops settled on their plantations here and there, evidencing to all the world, that instead of breathing the spirit of their office, they could, without remorse, *lay down their crown*, and bury the most important talents God has given men! We would rather choose that our episcopacy should be blotted out from the face of the earth, than be spotted with such disgraceful conduct! All the episcopal churches in the world are conscious of the dignity of their episcopal office. The greatest part of the endeavour to preserve this dignity by large salaries, splendid dresses, and other appendages of pomp and splendour. But if an episcopacy has neither the dignity which arises from these worldly trappings, nor that infinitely superior dignity which is the attendant of labour, of suffering and enduring hardship for the cause of Christ, and of a venerable old age, the concluding scene of a life, devoted to the service of God, it instantly becomes the disgrace of a church and the just ridicule of the world!

Some may think, that the mode of travelling, which the bishops are obliged to pursue, is attended with little difficulty, and much pleasure. Much pleasure they certainly do experience, because they know that they move in the will of God, and that the Lord is pleased to own their feeble labours. But if to travel through the heat and the cold, the rain and the snow, the swamps and the rivers, over mountains and through the wilderness, lying for nights together on the bare ground and in log-houses, open to the wind on every side, fulfilling their appointments, as far as possible, whatever be the hinderance,—if these be little difficulties, then our bishops have but little to endure.[14]

Bishops as itinerant general superintendents modeled and made work a very distinctive form of ministry, itinerancy.[15]

Issues

Well, what of today? What does traveling, what does itinerancy mean today? Who itinerates? in theory? in reality? What constitutes itinerancy today? How much of the traveling is with others and how much alone?

On first blush, one would be tempted to concede that itinerancy exists today in name only. Bishops have become increasingly local, even diocesan, most in North America serving a single conference, and many lingering for the allowed eight years and beyond. Pastorates follow this example of localization, especially in the larger churches. Longer pastorates also pertain in special situations, some ethnic appointments, and increasingly everywhere. Many United Methodists now pass along as received wisdom that longer appointments alone promise hope for effective and growing churches.

The real circuits—multiple-point charges—constitute the exception rather than the norm. They fall to persons in first appointment or to those in local or associate status or to student pastors. The station has become so much the norm that Methodist conversation now images ministry in stationary terms. Methodists now routinely speak of ministry as "parish." Appropriately, the *Discipline* apotheosizes the parish with a formal and stationary construct, that of "local church."[16] And the local church rather than bishop or conference determines salary, though to be sure bishop and cabinet can determine who will be the recipient of the salary set. Thus Methodists now tend to image the domain of ministry and people in static, self-contained, and even structural form.[17]

And what of the itinerancy from one appointment to the next, from circuit to circuit? Appointments grow longer and longer and have done so seemingly from the very beginning. Contemporary wisdom about church growth and leadership counsels yet even longer pastorates. Bishops and conferences go on record as committed to terms of eight or more years.[18] Reality contributes its own "counsel." Two career families and clergy couples position large proportions of a conference's membership in small orbits. Whole careers can be lived out within a district, or within a metropolitan area, or in alternating moves on and off the conference staff and cabinet. On the other hand, some ethnic and specialized ministries frequently demand considerable movement around a conference or even across conference lines.

Persons in ministry find themselves traveling in different circles, some small, some large. Subpopulations of clergy itinerate, by their own choice or by that of others, within tight boundaries. The boundaries or circles are defined by spousal employment, by common ethnicity of pastor and people, by the unwillingness of congregations to accept open itinerancy, by theological cliques, by family health considerations, and by education.[19] Others move across the entire conference. Quite different patterns of itinerancy, then, occur within a conference. Some ministers and congregations effectively opt out of the appointive and itinerant system. Class lines within the ministry seem as marked as those officially designated—between full and associate members, regular and extension appointees, elders and deacons.

The relation between ministerial conference membership and itinerancy has been altered by the 1996 *Discipline,* which establishes two distinct orders, removes the transitional diaconate, and permits a deacon considerable latitude in arranging his or her appointment and determining whether or not to itinerate. This change, creating a nonitinerant ordained ministry, though formally radical, effectively countenances for deacons what those in the relation termed "special," "appointments beyond the local church," or "extension ministries" have long enjoyed—namely a high degree of personal discretion in selecting and, ultimately, personal responsibility in locating employment.[20]

What, finally, of "the traveling together"? Is this aspect of itinerancy also imperiled? One might conclude that the image of lonely rider pertains far more today than it did in the days of Colbert. Annual conferences or clergy meetings assemble as many cars as they do people. Rarely do individuals carpool, even when long distances have to be traversed. Clergy want their vehicle in case an emergency beckons. They remain on call through beepers or cell phones. And they travel alone a lot—to local meetings, to the hospital, to shut-ins, to conference affairs.

And what about the other deeper meanings of itinerancy, including itinerancy as spiritual journeying. Does today's traveling alone deepen the inward and upward journey? What about itinerancy on the long road to perfection? What about itinerancy as itself a spiritual journey? Do ministers meditate as they go? They seem to destroy solitude and silence with a CD or tape player. The cynic might add that the pilgrimage "upward" today moves less along the path to perfection, notwithstanding the question posed by the bishop in ordination, and more along the trail marked by salary increases. Movement to an appointment with higher salary recognizes success, virtuosity, and accomplishment in ministry. Clergy compensation exposes other fault lines in itinerancy as well:

- wealthy churches persuading themselves and sometimes cabinets that they have a right to call or reappoint;
- whole populations of clergy maintained at "equitable" salary;
- appointment-making and appointment-monitoring highly observant of the salary issue;
- marked differences along lines of gender, race and ethnicity;
- morale issues being driven by and expressed in salary differentials.[21]

Related to these various strains and morale issues are worrisome dropout and burnout patterns, particularly in the first decade of ministry and among women.[22] The cynic might wonder whether dollars constitute the signposts on the *via salutis* rather than "doing no harm," "doing good," and "attending upon all the ordinances of God."

Bishops and cabinets remain nevertheless firmly committed to the ideal of itinerancy[23] and complain now, as they have since Asbury's day, that itinerancy has eroded. However, episcopal example does little to reinforce episcopal precept. The bishops themselves seem to want single conferences and want to remain settled for the full period permitted and beyond. Their "appointments" do not seem to model the itinerancy they would want of elders. They do, of course, travel nationally and globally on agency business or undertake spiritual excursions to the Holy Land.

If itinerancy is to be measured by sheer mobility, within an appointment and from appointment to appointment, if riding is the norm, then is itinerancy gone?

From Colbert to the Present

Itinerancy has clearly changed. Some of the change has been sought, legislated, and championed, for instance, the consultation that the *Discipline* now mandates. Other change has been unplanned, gradual, and only recognized after the fact. In recounting the evolution of Methodist ministry, our historians have been tempted, from the days of Wesley and Asbury on, to tell the story in jeremiadic terms, as one of declension. In the nineteenth century, Methodists had a regularly employed vehicle for such jeremiads and a class of individuals who regularly bemoaned the compromise of itinerancy. The latter were called croakers.[24] Their jeremiadic account of Methodist betrayal of its ideals and its decline found most eloquent expression in an established genre, the semi-centennial sermon, preached by an old-timer on his fiftieth year in the traveling ministry. It was indeed a stylized rhetorical form, a genre. The preacher routinely celebrated the ministry of his youth, the hardships faced, the souls won, the high standards maintained, the doctrine exemplified. He then bemoaned the ease, sloth, low standards, and error of the day.

To avoid the jeremiadic temptation, to tell the story as one of evolution not declension, involves recognizing change as inevitable.[25] Much of the change in itinerancy tracks change in Methodism itself, in North American society, and in Methodism's place therein. Growing membership in a community demanded larger places for gathering, and Methodist prominence among the denominations of a community called for a building to symbolize that leadership. A churchlike building, in turn, invited ministry to settle into station roles, and a parsonage invited longer settlements (appointments). The station appointment gradually became the norm, a shift finally captured in the twentieth century in the Disciplinary emphasis upon "the local church."

Mission dictated change. Effective evangelism required, so thought Nathan Bangs and others, a continuous pastoral presence to harvest what revivals yielded. Also, as the movement gained adherents among or encouraged its adherents into the middling classes, Methodist laity wanted stable, trained, effective, available local pastoral leadership, not quarterly or biweekly visits of a self-educated preacher. So the denomination began to stretch the term of appointments. It elaborated better training processes—first the course of study, then colleges, and eventually seminaries. It abandoned the common salary, which gave way first on missional grounds and in recognition of higher cost appointments and then as an expression of a charge's ability and willingness to "reward" its minister. Thus unfolded the long process by which the traveling preachers became parish ministers.[26]

The commissioned nature of itinerancy, expressed in conference membership, created theological quandaries for Methodism that, one might argue, it has never satisfactorily solved but that occasioned concession and resistance, both moves productive of change. Quandaries over conference membership helped produce a major schism, that between the Methodist Protestants and Methodist Episcopacy. One of the dynamics in that division was what the church would do with the steady departure from the itinerancy and from conference of preachers who chose to locate, often for family and financial reasons. Those "locating," Bishop Asbury complained, were among the "brightest ornaments" of the church. Many local preachers had indeed had distinguished itinerant careers. Others became local preachers temporarily on their way to itinerancy. Still others became local preachers with little prospect of ever being able to travel. For much of the nineteenth century, local preachers constituted two thirds of the active ministerial leadership of Methodism. Did their numbers, experience, role, and work warrant voice, status, and suffrage in annual and general conference, that is, in those bodies within which ministry symbolized itself and where decisions were made and legislation passed for the church? (The reformers whose concerns produced Methodist Protestantism also complained that the laity were excluded from the decision-making process.) Issues of the power and authority of local preachers, of their sacramental authority, of elders' orders, and of the representation of the communities they served all inhered in the question of conference membership. At one time or another, such thorny problems complicated themselves further with dynamics of race, gender, language, and class. For instance, African Americans withdrew to form their own communion when the Methodist Episcopal Church refused to advance their ministerial leadership (particularly that of Richard Allen) beyond the level of "local" deacon.

Various aspirations for inclusion in, enlargement of, or transformation of the itinerancy, the Methodist Episcopal Church often resisted, only eventually to grant. The efforts at preservation or resistance changed ministry, as did the more obvious reforms. The MEC rebuffed

- efforts to provide for an appeal of an appointment;
- African American aspirations for full ordination and conference membership;
- campaigns for election of presiding elders and for representation of local preachers and laity;
- pleas for ordination of women and for inclusion of women in General Conference.

From these rebuffs, over the course of the nineteenth century, came repeated divisions and internal strains. Also affected were the flexibility, fluidity, and opportunity of itinerancy. Defensive and boundary-establishing efforts made the itinerancy into a closed fraternity, a white male bastion. Denominational divisions and legislated ethnic and central conferences created alternative "fraternities" for Methodism's racial and linguistic communities. Eventually the several Methodist denominations found space for women in the itinerancy. However, the long, defensive campaigns against opening itinerancy to those showing effective leadership in the life of the community produced patterns of "clericalism."[27]

Systemic forces clericalized itinerancy. Systemic forces also regionalized it. The bounding of itinerancy within annual conferences began early but proceeded slowly. When bishops genuinely itinerated over the entire church, covered multiple conferences annually and received yet a different set of conference appointments each year, they [the bishops] routinely and reflexively solved special problems or met special opportunities by thinking connectionally and transferring, when needed, a minister from one conference over which they had presided to another. The slow evolution of the episcopacy from an itinerating to a more localized, even diocesan-like, institution made the transfer of ministers across conference lines increasingly rare and made the itinerancy a conference—that is, a regional affair. To that development, other factors contributed as well, among them,

- the establishment of conference boundaries and therefore of clear membership in a conference,
- the creation of the delegated general conference, which made continued membership and the development of a following or constituency essential to national prominence,

- the gradual adjustment of conference lines to those of the states,
- the key role that cabinets (early termed councils)—that is, intra-conference connections—played in appointments,
- the authority and power that conferences exercised in the admissions and credentialing processes,
- and the sheer power of regionalism in American life.

All these made more and more exceptional the cross-fertilization and questioning and stimulation that came from bringing experience, expertise, and special gifts from outside.

The confining of itinerancy within conference ironically paved the way in the twentieth century for conferences to behave for their members as a professional organization.[28] Conferences undertook for ministers what the AMA and ABA did for doctors and lawyers:

- establishing, maintaining, defending, and upgrading standards;
- serving credentialing functions and determining who would be admitted;
- worrying over working and living conditions (parsonages);
- lobbying for minimum salary protections and higher salary possibilities;
- pressing for adequate pension, insurance, and medical coverage;
- exercising ethical oversight and encouraging professional etiquette;
- and, in general, defending ministerial prerogative.

Conference exercise of these responsibilities required some dexterity because during the same period that they came to exercise professional roles conferences also admitted laity (MECS [1854], UB [1872], EA [1907], MC [1939]). Conferences found ways, through committees or boards of ministry, to accommodate professionalism while becoming ever more representative in plenary session. In consequence, itinerancy as the mode or form of Methodist ministry also took on professional aspects. Not surprising perhaps were the tendencies to measure effectiveness in ministry by those hallmarks or signs of professional advancement—salary, status of assignment, size of constituency, stability in appointment. Itinerancy became less a journey and a way of life and more a status and an office.

What then of itinerancy?

The Journey Ahead

Perhaps more important than sheer mobility, than riding in and of itself, are the ends, the purposes, the mission served by riding and attendant factors that went into riding. Perhaps, in thinking about itinerancy, we have focused too much on mobility itself and on its privileged image "the lonely rider" and not thought enough on the "how and where" of riding, and on the "with whom," and on the "to what" destination(s). In rethinking let us return to the rubrics extracted and elaborated from the vignette of William Colbert—corporate, yoked, sent, appointed and appointing, covenanted, commissioned, connected—and note also the several spiritual movements—upward, onward, inward, outward, around—that itinerancy entailed.

What then about contemporary ministry and that of the future? First, we should acknowledge and celebrate the expectations for more corporate expression of ministry offered by the 1996 and subsequent *Disciplines* through covenants for orders of deacons and elders, and for covenants during the probationary period. Underlying these new provisions are the practices of covenanting and covenant discipleship within the Council and Colleges of Bishops, and the efforts made by David Lowes Watson and colleagues to reclaim covenant discipleship within the denomination.[29] Those commissioned, the *Discipline* expects to be involved in covenant groups for the entire journey of their probation. And that bonding, many hope, will carry on past ordination. The small covenant groups during probation should also leaven the covenants being established within the two orders, elders and deacon.

Second, probation also is to involve serious mentoring, yoking of an experienced practitioner with the neophyte. Some conferences have been successfully employing mentors already, as have some theological schools in field education programs. And those involved with diaconal ministry have also played or experienced such roles. Patterns of yoking have existed, at least informally, among women coming into ministry and within some ethnic communities. However, both mentoring and covenanting will not fundamentally reshape the ministry as a whole unless new itinerants survive the probationary period and somehow overcome the patterns of competition, mistrust, and isolation that persist among the itinerants (elders especially). Can trust, openness, confidentiality be sustained when ministers wonder and worry whether colleagues might end up as their district superintendents?

Third, real trust can, we think, be engendered by and also engender our reclaiming and recreating the missionary and connectional understandings of itinerancy and identification of its appointive character in such purposive terms. The larger, evangelical meaning of our itinerancy requires our thinking of it theologically in some counterpart of the multiple themes exegeted in relation to the Colbert vignette.

Fourth, itinerancy also might be reinvigorated by our imagining twenty-first-century counterparts to the spiritual journeying that early preachers experienced on horseback. Perhaps motifs of movement from Emmaus Walk, from retreats, or from the use of labyrinths as a spiritual discipline might be drawn upon for some respiritualization of the journeys of today's ministers. Might there be particular disciplines of meditation for the morning ride to church, for the walk into the building, for excursions down church hallways, for drives to nursing home or hospital, for journeys to conference events? How might the rhythms of everyday ministry, including the time spent in the car, be again made pilgrimage?

Fifth, the category or ritual act of commissioning offers promise, if given some serious theological attention. United Methodism continues the worry over its understanding of ministry and how to symbolize, empower, train, and authorize the range of ministerial roles and offices that it needs and creates. The church still puzzles over the status of the local pastor. It has resolved problems that the office of diaconal ministry posed with the new permanent deacon and the establishment of deacon and elder orders. The decision to "commission" probationers for both orders seemed at first to be a theological and ecumenical misstep. By conferring sacramental authority to those commissioned on the elder track, it regularizes what other communions find to be an ecclesial and sacramental scandal, namely celebration of the Eucharist by non-presbyters (local preachers and student pastors already posing the problem). Are there ways to think about commissioning in some fresh ways, in relation to ordination and conference membership and the mission of the church?

Sixth, the modeling by the bishops of covenanting together in small groups, raising their spiritual ambitions and collectively assuming service, outreach, or justice commitments should prove helpful in actualizing the 1996 provisions. The bishops, I think one could show, have patterned ministry for Methodism. Their individual and collective efforts at disciplined, purposive, covenanted spirituality can do much for many of the significant, deeper meanings of itinerancy.

Seventh, what most needs reaffirmation is the understanding of ministry as sent, appointive, missionary, apostolic. Here episcopal example may hurt more than it helps. Superintendents the bishops certainly are. But neither they nor the church seem as eager as they might be to exploit fully their "itinerant" or "general" calling. And they as much as the preachers politick for longer appointments. Nor are the sent, appointive, and missionary dimensions of itinerancy and conference membership invigorated by the swelling numbers of those of us in extension capacity.

Perhaps we will only recover an itinerant elder if we clarify the role of those in these special appointments. Many of us—in chaplaincies, campus ministries, seminary teaching positions, and administrative positions—genuinely need ordination and sacramental authority. Some of us do not need guaranteed appointments or conference membership. Perhaps it is time to reclaim one of the historic uses of the local elder. For much of the nineteenth century, two dynamics produced local preachers, as we have just noted. Then as now many came into the office from other leadership roles in a community and were not in a position to exercise leadership beyond that locale. Others located after effective, indeed, often distinguished ministries, sometimes in connectional leadership. If the local elder was rethought and those of us in "extension" roles invited to locate or in some other way to remove ourselves from the appointive ranks, perhaps we would be clearer that persons appointed—however long they had been so—were sent. Alternatively, those in extension ministries might be authorized to transfer into some newly created conference entity, perhaps a central conference, where the accountability and mission of those offices were given special attention. Either way, United Methodism could reaffirm the essential point about itinerancy, that it has fundamentally to do not with travel nor with the duration of a pastoral post, but with an apostolic understanding of the ministerial office.

Understanding Itinerancy Scripturally

Itinerancy we have seen has always been about something more than a man and a horse, about more than travel, about more than being moved in ministry. It constituted a complex metaphor for a multifaceted ministry, a variety of journeys, and a corporate itinerancy—ministry carried on connectionally, as much with one's peers as apart from them. Itinerancy was communal, cooperative, missionary or evangelical, appointed/appointive/under authority, connectional, commissioned, covenantal, a spiritual journeying.

Various dimensions and forms of ministry derive from or are warranted by Scripture. The Wesleyan understanding of ministry draws heavily upon the example of the disciples, of the apostle Paul, and of Jesus himself. This point Francis Asbury made repeatedly, in insisting on the "apostolic" nature of itinerancy. Sustaining this point, both bishops, Thomas Coke and Francis Asbury, cited Scripture liberally in their annotated *The Doctrines and Discipline* (1798). The Methodist conception of itinerancy is not and has never been just a denominational way, an organizational style, a human relations system, a ministerial management or deployment program. Nor is it a matter of inertia, precedent, mechanics, or pragmatism. Methodists have a very scriptural, particularly Pauline and Johannine, theology of ministry, one rooted in the command of Jesus, the pattern of Paul's ministry, and the self-understanding of Jesus according to the Gospel of John.

First, Wesleyan understandings take seriously the ministerial pattern into which Jesus invited, or better, commanded the disciples. In Mark's account, Jesus commissioned, appointed, sent the disciples, two-by-two—a pattern later adopted by early Methodists.

> Then Jesus went around teaching from village to village. Calling the Twelve to him, *he sent them out two by two* and gave them authority over evil spirits. These were his instructions: "Take nothing for the journey except a staff—no bread, no bag, no money in your belts. Wear sandals but not an extra tunic. Whenever you enter a house, stay there until you leave that town. And if any place will not welcome you or listen to you, shake the dust off your feet when you leave, as a testimony against them." They went out and preached that people should repent. They drove out many demons and anointed many sick people with oil and healed them. (Mark 6:7-13, emphasis added)

In Luke's version, Jesus sends and commissions disciples more generally, as the seventy (or seventy-two):

> After this the Lord *appointed seventy-two others and sent them two by two* ahead of him to every town and place where he was about to go. He told them, "The harvest is plentiful, but the workers are few. Ask the Lord of the harvest, therefore, to send out workers into his harvest field. Go! I am sending you out like lambs among wolves." (Luke 10:1-3, emphasis added)

Paul as well as the various evangelists reported in Acts exemplify the itinerant pattern. Paul's own letters offer rich resources for the understanding of itinerancy. But perhaps the most powerful witness to itinerancy can be found in the Gospel of John. There Jesus explicitly proclaims discipleship, faithfulness, ministry to be "sent." In two places he does so explicitly:

> Again Jesus said, "Peace be with you! As the Father has sent me, I am sending you." (John 20:21)

> As you sent me into the world, I have sent them into the world. For them I sanctify myself, that they too may be truly sanctified. "My prayer is not

for them alone. I pray also for those who will believe in me through their message, that all of them may be one, Father, just as you are in me and I am in you. May they also be in us so that the world may believe that you have sent me. I have given them the glory that you gave me, that they may be one as we are one: I in them and you in me. May they be brought to complete unity to let the world know that you sent me and have loved them even as you have loved me." (John 17:18-23)

In John, Jesus sends into ministry as he himself was sent. Throughout that Gospel, Jesus represents his own ministry as "sent," repeatedly referring to "the Father who sent me." Being "sent" by Jesus makes our ministry quite truly representative—and we can bemoan the purging of that notion of representative ministry from the *Discipline*. Representative ministry norms itself on that of Jesus, of being sent by Jesus as Jesus was sent by the Father.

So itinerancy does, indeed, have less to do with mechanics than with theology. Implicit in itinerancy lie profound understandings of the gospel, of church, and of the ministry. Itinerancy—and the next move, and the next one after that—have to do fundamentally with how Methodists understand God to work in the world. God works by sending. Itinerancy is a biblical and apostolic form of ministry.

Conclusion

So when the D.S. calls a clergy family or the staff relations committee with an announcement of reappointment, as the D.S. most certainly will, what should be the response? Well, one cannot help the upset and resentment over having to move or having a beloved pastor moved. But should not one think both about the current charge and its pastor and the place of both within a missionary order and a connection? The D.S. who calls acts on behalf of the connection, presuming that both minister and spouse serve communally and cooperatively with all under appointment, that Methodists understand ministries, even the joint ministries of pastor and spouse, to be fundamentally missionary in nature, and that preachers are to embrace this next charge as part of a larger spiritual journey.

The same theological self-understanding belongs more explicitly to the office of the itinerant general superintendents, the bishops, whom Methodists have expected, since Wesley and Asbury, to model our form of apostolic ministry.

Why itinerancy? Because it is the Methodist pattern? Because Mr. Wesley embraced and institutionalized it? Because Francis Asbury imposed it by precept, command, and example? Because we have always done it that way? Because it functions as well as alternative systems? Because it worked/works? Because it effectively deploys ministers, guarantees every pastor a church and every church a minister?

No. United Methodists adhere to itinerancy as an apostolic plan, as an institutional hearing of what the apostle Paul said as indeed counsel to us personally.

CHAPTER THREE

Disciplined, Disciplining

1 TWO are better far than one[1]
For counsel or for fight;
How can one be warm alone,
Or serve his God aright?
Join we then our hearts and hands,
Each to love provoke his friend;
Run the way of his commands,
And keep it to the end.

2 Woe to him whose spirits droop,
To him who falls alone!
He has none to lift him up,
To help his weakness on:
Happier we each other keep,
We each other's burdens bear;
Never need our footsteps slip,
Upheld by mutual prayer.

3 Who of twain hath made us one,
Maintains our unity,
Jesus is the corner-stone,
In whom we all agree;
Servants of one common Lord,
Sweetly of one heart and mind,
Who can break a threefold cord,
Or part whom God hath joined?

4 O that all with us might prove
The fellowship of saints!
Find supplied, in Jesu's love,
What every member wants:
Grasp we our high calling's prize,
Feel our sins on earth forgiven,
Rise, in his whole image rise,
And meet our Head in heaven!

To most United Methodists, I suspect, the word "discipline" if used in church circles would be understood to refer to a book. They would know, even if they do not possess a current one, or for that matter have ever held one in their hands, that United Methodism runs itself by the *Discipline*. And they would have a pretty good sense that their pastor, the District Superintendent, the Bishop, and other representatives of United Methodist officialdom take this book with some seriousness. Perhaps they would have heard frequent references to the *Discipline* in a church or charge conference and would have seen it beside the pastor or D.S. in hymnal-like size, shape, and binding. Should they have attended an annual conference, they would know that bishops have an extraordinarily high regard for the *Discipline* and make rulings on its authority. If they have followed church controversies in the press, they would know that structures, codes, regulations, laws, and doctrines in that book can be and are fought over, indeed, can occasion defrocking of clergy and perhaps even denominational division. Despite such awareness, they would have seldom if ever had an encouragement to look into, much less purchase this volume. *Discipline,* as far as they were concerned, could remain the preacher's and bishop's book.

Few United Methodists would know that others in the Wesleyan or Methodist family have a similar official but ambivalent relation to this word and a book so designated. Nor would they have much idea of discipline as a shared preoccupation across Christianity, indeed as one of the defining concerns of the church. They probably would not connect the word with exercises or activities of the church in earlier eras.

Methodists gave the name discipline to their book not because it could mean so little but because it meant so much. It served several different parts of Methodist speech. It functioned as noun, verb, adverb, adjective. It referred to a book, an exercise of ecclesiastical judgment, a way of living, a set of practices, loving mutuality in oversight, a recognized accountability, the state or act of being faithful to the gospel, the good order of the church, and therefore the polity or governance of the church.

An act of discipline by Bishop Melvin G. Talbert invites our exploration of its meanings.

Vignette

Bishop Talbert Announces Complaint Against 69 Pastors

STATEMENT[2] On Jan. 16, 1999, a number of clergy participated in a holy union celebration at the Sacramento Convention Center. These clergy celebrated a covenant between Ellie Charlton and Jeanne Barnett, two well-known and respected members of Sacramento St. Mark's United Methodist Church, where the Rev. Donald Fado is pastor. Ellie and Jeanne are leaders beyond their local congregation. Ellie is a member of the Conference Board of Trustees. Jeanne is conference lay leader, one of the most influential offices held by a lay person in our denomination. Jeanne was also elected a delegate to our General Conference, the highest legislative body of our denomination. Ellie and Jeanne are honorable, loyal and dedicated followers of Jesus Christ. Like other Christians, they are living out their faith in the name and spirit of Jesus Christ.

With such affirmation of these two persons, why are we here today? We are here because Ellie and Jeanne are homosexuals. They have chosen to be public in their commitment to each other. They sought and received the blessing of their church by the action of their pastor, and others, who chose to officiate at their public celebration.

For a variety of reasons, homosexuality has been and continues to be a very controversial subject in society and in churches, especially in our denomination. Some would draw the circle of full membership to include homosexuals without judgment. Others would limit their church participation and prohibit their full involvement. Thus, we have the continuing debate, especially around the issue of holy unions.

The celebration of holy unions is not new in our denomination. This has been going on for decades. What makes this different is the action taken at our General Conference in 1996, which states: "Ceremonies that celebrate homosexual unions shall not be conducted by our ministers and shall not be conducted in our churches" (Paragraph 65.C, *1996 Book of Discipline of The United Methodist Church*).

This language is very clear. However, a problem was created by the placement of that language in the *Book of Discipline*. It was placed in the section called "The Social Principles." As stated in the preface, "The Social Principles are a prayerful and thoughtful effort on the part of the General Conference to speak to the human issues in the contemporary world from a sound biblical and theological foundation as historically demonstrated in United Methodist traditions. They are intended to be instructive and persuasive in the best of the prophetic spirit. The Social Principles are a call to all members of the United Methodist Church to a prayerful, studied dialogue of faith and practice."

In short, the Social Principles are not law. They have not been treated as such since the beginning of our denomination more than 200 years ago. And when asked to interpret this action of General Conference, I did so in the best tradition of our church. I indicated that such action was not law, and to violate that action would not constitute grounds for a chargeable offense. That interpretation set off a storm of controversy in this conference and in our denomination. Some went so far as to demand that I resign from my office as bishop. Of course, I did not resign.

As a result of the Jimmy Creech case in Nebraska (he was acquitted after being tried for celebrating a holy union), my bishop colleagues in the South Central Jurisdiction appealed to the Judicial Council, the highest court in our denomination. Those bishops, and others, presented the argument that the intention of the General Conference was to enact a law to prohibit the celebration of homosexual unions. In August 1998, the Judicial Council ruled in favor of those who argued that the intent of General Conference was to enact a law. So the Judicial Council ruling states: "The prohibitive statement in Paragraph 65.C of the *1996 Book of Discipline:* 'Ceremonies that celebrate homosexual unions shall not be conducted by our ministers and shall not be conducted in our churches,' has the effect of church law, notwithstanding its placement in Paragraph 65.C and, therefore, governs the conduct of the ministerial office. Conduct in violation of this prohibition renders a pastor liable to a charge of disobedience to the order and discipline of the United Methodist Church under Paragraph 2624 of the Discipline."

When this ruling was released, I expressed my sorrow and disappointment with it. However, as a bishop of the church, I stated that I would abide by the decision and uphold it, even though I disagreed with it. Now, I could have run for cover by using the law as a basis for remaining silent on this issue. In a sense the matter of law is settled. But my conscience wouldn't allow me to take the easy way out. I had to speak out against this act of injustice. So I will uphold the law, but I will not be silenced. I will continue speaking out against the law and will continue working to change the position of our church to be more in keeping with the teachings and compassion of Jesus. That is the position I stated in my Jan. 6 pastoral letter to clergy and lay members of the California-Nevada Conference. I further stated my personal belief that the position taken by our church on this issue is wrong, because such action infringes on the sacred pastoral role of one as priest and servant. I reaffirm that position today. I agree with those pastors who contend that such action is an intrusion into their priestly role as clergy to all their people.

Clergy are called on to do many things. They baptize children and adults. They bless homes, instruments, cars, parks, fowls, animals, buildings and various type events. In all such occasions, clergy persons are free to choose whether they will or will not perform such services. Yet when it comes to this one event of a holy union, it is prohibited. This is unconscionable! I contend that all clergy must be free to choose the appropriate pastoral responses they should make in the priestly roles. This must never become a political action. Today, it is homosexuality. What will the next issue be? Do you remember when the issue was race?

Thus, the debate continues in society and in our churches. There are honorable people on both sides of this issue, which could split our church. In the face of such controversy, there is need for tolerance. I believe this is such a time when honorable Christians can agree to disagree, without allowing such an issue to separate us from God's table. The gospel of Jesus Christ reminds me that all sinners are invited to God's table. That being true, who, other than God, can decide to exclude some? Therefore, I refuse to treat as enemies those who chose to violate this church law, as an act of conscience. They are not our enemies. They are our sisters and brothers in Christ, in the same way that those are who hold opposing views. Biblical and theological debates are appropriate. But there comes a time when God's call to love must take precedence over any political or theological action or decision. I believe that is the case now with this issue. I will continue proclaiming that we all belong to God, and that we will have a space at God's table. Praise God!

However, it is my responsibility to announce that on this day, March 23, 1999, a complaint, signed by the Rev. Ardith Allread, dean of the cabinet, and by the Rev. David Bennett, superintendent for the district where the Jan. 16th event was held, has been presented to me listing the names of 69 persons. The complaint states, "These clergy persons, who claimed their participation was an act of conscience and pastoral ministry, acted in violation of the Judicial Council ruling with regard to Paragraph 65.C of the *1996 Book of Discipline.* According to the ruling, these clergy persons failed to uphold the order and discipline of the United Methodist Church."

The complaint further states: "The bishop and the cabinet, through the supervisory process as outlined in Paragraph 358.1 of the *1996 Book of Discipline,* have attempted to reach resolution in the matter. Each district superintendent met with those persons who officiated at the service of holy union. Some plans for possible ways to achieve resolution were lifted up. None of the plans were acceptable to the persons listed in this complaint. Therefore, resolution was not achieved."

These two district superintendents conclude the complaint, stating, " . . . despite our theological and pastoral disagreement with this area of church law, a complaint of disobedience to the order and discipline of The United Methodist Church (Paragraph 2624.1(e) of the *1996 Book of Discipline*) is filed against the following clergy . . . " (listed in original statement).

As a bishop of the church, I have accepted this complaint from my colleagues. I join them in stating I personally disagree with this area of church law. Nevertheless, it is my intention to refer to this complaint as a judicial complaint to the counsel for the church pursuant to Paragraph 358.1 of the *1996 Book of Discipline.* The person I have appointed as counsel for the church is the Rev. Paul Wiberg, pastor, St. Mark's United Methodist Church, Orinda, Calif. It will be his responsibility to sign the complaint and forward the same to the Conference Committee on Investigation. If that committee sees fit to do so, it may turn the complaint into charges which may result in a trial. And if or when that happens, I shall be prepared to convene a pool of 35 or more elders appointed by the district superintendents, from which a jury will be selected. And, I will place the charges in the hands of a colleague bishop of my choosing who will preside over the trial.

This is a very painful day for me. The persons on both sides of this issue are my sisters and brothers. They are faithful followers of Jesus Christ. Yet, there are honest differences in opinions regarding this controversial issue in our church. Those colleagues named in this complaint have chosen to challenge this unjust law. I understand their wishes. I am a disciple of the civil rights protests. From my own experiences, I can appreciate acts of conscience and acts of civil disobedience. Therefore, my referring this complaint is without prejudice to enable these colleagues to have their day in a court of peers. My prayer is that in the due process to follow, clergy peers will seek to do justice, and to act in a way that is consistent with the teachings and compassion of Jesus. I trust they will hold before them the vision for our church that is inclusive, with diversity and acceptance as its hallmarks. May God bless all of us as we seize this moment as an opportunity to model how Christians should deal with controversy in our lives and in our churches.

Commentary

This ruling and statement by Bishop Melvin G. Talbert illustrates something of the richness and nuance in United Methodism's understanding of discipline. The term defies quick definition. It serves several different parts of Methodist speech. It functions as noun, verb, adverb, adjective. It can refer to a book, an exercise of ecclesiastical judgment, a way of living, a set of practices, loving mutuality in oversight, a recognized accountability, the state or act of being faithful to the gospel, the good order of the church, and the polity or governance of the church.

First, it refers to a book,[3] in this particular instance the *1996 Book of Discipline of The United Methodist Church,* with whose pronouncement on the matter of homosexual unions Bishop Talbert struggles. Under this book Methodists have, one might argue, lived from the beginning. The Discipline derived from John Wesley's "Large Minutes," one of the several norms for early Methodism, along with his *Explanatory Notes Upon the New Testament* and *Sermons on Several Occasions.* Wesley had distilled "The Large Minutes" out of the questions and answers by which he, in successive conferences with his preachers, had hammered out the doctrines, practices, expectations, and procedures by which the movement would live.

When, in 1784, Mr. Wesley recognized the "very uncommon train of Providences" that had disengaged the provinces from English political and ecclesial dominion, he set them "at full liberty, simply to follow the Scriptures and the Primitive Church."[4] Exercising that liberty cautiously, the gathering of preachers known as the Christmas Conference adapted the 1780 version of "The Large Minutes" for American usage. The first edition of what would thereafter be called the *Discipline* bore in its title a statement of the transition: *Minutes of Several Conversations between the Rev. Thomas Coke, LL.D., The Rev. Francis Asbury and Others, At a Conference, Begun in Baltimore, in the State of Maryland, on Monday, the 27th of December, in the Year 1784. Composing a Form of Discipline for the Ministers, Preachers and Other Members of the Methodist Episcopal Church in America.*[5] One can readily recognize the dependence of the *Discipline* on the "Large Minutes" by inspecting the two in parallel columns nicely provided by John J. Tigert in *A Constitutional History of American Episcopal Methodism.*[6] There one can see that the church, that is, the Methodist Episcopal Church, constituted itself in the adaptation of Wesley's "Large Minutes" into a *Discipline.* They did so, adding, deleting, amending as appropriate for American circumstances and for a new church in a new nation.

Thereafter *Discipline* would refer to this book by which the Methodist movement in its various permutations and combinations would live. Both the United Brethren and the Evangelical Association also created Disciplines, the latter actually employing a German translation of the Methodist's as template.[7] The African Methodists effected their own translations, as Michael Cartwright shows, translations that served as commentary on the ethical failures of white Methodism.[8] Typically, as well, the responsibility for updating and amending the *Discipline* would be lodged in the church's plenary body, its General Conference. Might just such a further updating and amendment of "discipline" and the *Discipline* be implicit in Bishop Talbert's sustained argument against the "discipline" he feels constrained to exercise?

This brings us **secondly** to the juridical meaning of the term, to Talbert's exercise of discipline. He finds himself as bishop, as member of the Council of Bishops, as one in their covenant, as one respecting the prior ruling of the Judicial Council obliged to bring a number of clergy under charges "of disobedience to the order and discipline of The United Methodist Church under ¶ 2624 of the *Discipline*" for their concelebration of a homosexual union. Complaint having been registered, procedures followed, Talbert makes preparations for a juried trial.

Until this issue brought them back, trials and similar exercises of judgment had largely fallen into disuse. They had once been a common feature of Methodist life at all levels.[9] Classes existed primarily to exercise discipline in this sense. Quarterly conferences heard appeals from class-level discipline and exercised disciplinary oversight over those particularly accountable to it, most notably local preachers. Appeals from quarterly conference could be made to annual conference. Annual conferences spent much of their long sittings in disciplining their own members, in the review of character by which every traveling preacher, every year, had his name individually called and his character subjected to review (and it was "his" for a long time). One's trial by annual-scrutiny-of-peers passed quickly except when malfeasance subjected the individual to "arrest" and then regular and gradually refined juridical procedures followed. And when the church established general conferences, appeal could be made from the annual conference level. The powers to receive appeals and to review the constitutionality of other juridical as well as legislative actions have, since the unions of 1939 and 1968, been lodged in the Judicial Council.

The provision for formal trials of members, preachers, *and* superintendents and for some form of peer juries was an American addition to "The Large Minutes."[10] And trials were, as indicated, a regular feature of early Methodist life. However, formal trials constituted a minor part of the exercise of discipline, and all Methodist life was, in a sense, "on trial." Members as well as preachers entered through a probationary state, in the case of the former structurally represented by inclusion in a probationary class. Movement to a regular class changed only the kind of probation under which members lived, namely under the rules of the *Discipline* and with quarterly redetermination of their good standing through the issuance of tickets. Holding a ticket gained one access to the sacramental and organizational life of Methodism, in particular to Society, love feast, and the Lord's Supper. Rules guiding class leaders and preachers in the exercise of such "discipline" constituted a major portion of early *Disciplines*.[11]

Another major portion of the *Discipline* gave guidance to those attempting to live under discipline. This brings us to the **third** meaning of the word. A disciplined life—the Methodist way begun with the Holy Club—has "marked" the Methodist. Being Methodist has meant discipline and self-discipline and disciplined living.[12] In the vignette above, Talbert seems to recognize the disciplined life of the couple, Ellie Charlton and Jeanne Barnett, their being "honorable, loyal and dedicated followers of Jesus Christ," as warranting a bond and a ceremony which the *1996 Book of Discipline* proscribes. He might have cited an interesting precedent for ministers honoring such disciplined life by conducting "illegal" and "civilly disobedient" ceremonies. In the antebellum South, preachers were charged and tried for conducting marriages of slaves where the laws forbade such "illegal unions." There, too, expectations of "discipline" clashed.

Such clashes derive from tensions that Wesleyan disciplines create with everyday life and worldly patterns. Mr. Wesley's rules called for behavior and proscribed behavior at points very much counter to business practices and genteel society. The disciplined life to which Methodists would be held accountable embraced various codes of care for one another, for others, and for oneself—one such dimension of which we return to below. Among the rules that sharply distinguished Methodists in early American society were those on dress and slavery. In 1784, the Methodist Episcopal Church added to "The Large Minutes" rules calculated to end connection of Methodists with slavery. The *Discipline* asked:

> Q. 42. What Methods can we take to extirpate Slavery?
>
> A. We are deeply conscious of the Impropriety of making new Terms of Communion for a religious Society already established, excepting on the most pressing Occasion: and such we esteem the Practice of holding our Fellow-Creatures in Slavery. We view it as contrary to the Golden Law of God on which hang all Law and the Prophets, and the unalienable Rights of Mankind, as well as every Principle of the Revolution, to hold in the deepest Debasement, in a more abject Slavery than is perhaps to be found in any Part of the World except America, so many Souls that are all capable of the Image of God.

Then followed provisions for manumission, buttressed with the sanction of excommunication but qualified most regrettably by the concession that

> these Rules are to affect the Members of our Society no further than as they are consistent with the Laws of the States in which they reside.
>
> And respecting our Brethren in *Virginia* that are concerned, and after due Consideration if their peculiar Circumstances, we allow them two Years from the Notice given, to consider the Expedience of Compliance or Non-Compliance with these Rules.

The first *Discipline* served notice that being Methodist required a disciplined life. However, it also recognized that its expectations could and did run counter to worldly practices and that not all who had heard Methodist preaching and found themselves drawn to Methodist community could live by Methodist standards:

In Consideration that these Rules form a new Term of Communion, every Person concerned, who will not comply with them, shall have Liberty quietly to withdraw himself from our Society within the twelve Months succeeding the Notice given as aforesaid: Otherwise the Assistant shall exclude him in the Society.[13]

The rules on slavery conformed nicely to those myriad rules for the holy life derived from Wesley that set Methodist life in angular relation to the world. Black Methodists maintained those rules and kept that angularity. White Methodists in the South found themselves being selective in their adherence and accommodating their disciplines to slavery and later to segregation.[14] Eventually white Southerners found themselves in a quandary similar to Talbert's. Separate disciplinary expectations against slavery, of marriage as a human norm, and of adherence to slave codes prohibiting slave marriages clashed.

Rules for Christian living—rules addressed to members, rules for members but addressed to class leaders, or rules for members but addressed to preachers—constituted the vast bulk of early Disciplines. These historic rules and the disciplined life to which the Methodist was obliged are given in a brief and retrospective rendering in the current *Discipline*.[15] The *Discipline* was a book to be lived with. The preachers were said to be people of three books—Bible, Hymnal, and *Discipline*. And the people were much the same. However, patterns of disciplined living among Methodists changed significantly in the nineteenth century and not just on slavery.[16] Many urban and middle-class Methodists came to experience the codes on dress and jewelry and other measures for a plain and frugal life as legalistic, not spiritually uplifting. Other sectors of the church perceived those codes to have enduring value and to be expressive of the Wesleyan quest for holiness. Some of these holiness adherents took such disciplines to be Methodist essentials and finally separated themselves to remain faithful (Wesleyans, Free Methodists).

Still, disciplined living continued well into the twentieth century in the two Methodist Episcopal churches, perhaps most dramatically in the communal life of deaconesses, in the Methodist settlement houses, and in regulations concerning drinking and smoking.[17] Deaconesses exemplified life lived fully under Methodist ideals—committing themselves to selfless service, living in community, following detailed rules, and adopting garb that distinguished them. The settlement movement, various other reform initiatives, and missions, domestic and global also attested high resolve for the disciplined life. The "discipline" that Methodists made the law of the land, temperance, represented a courageous witness and one that non-Methodists seem more eager than we to recall as "marking" the movement. Prohibition attested Methodist commitment to rules by which we thought a whole society could and should live. Others joined this cause but the WCTU and the Saloon League were our institutions and neither state nor national legislation would have passed without the lobbying of our bishops, preachers, and women. Long after repeal the temperance discipline lived on as a ministerial expectation. The shibboleth for ordination was a vow against smoking and drinking. And today, persons seeking ordination respond in examination to questions prefaced by the exhortation, "are you willing to make a complete dedication of yourself to the highest ideals of the Christian life," and in the ordination ritual to queries put as the "Historic Examination for Admission into Full Connection and Ordination."

The historic questions some may find quaint, but it is the expectation that clergy (and the people called Methodist) live a disciplined life, honor their covenants and commitments, adhere to codes of ethics. And the moral life remains crucially important in United Methodism as in other Christian communion, however one comes down on the thicket of issues that Talbert faced.

The rules for disciplined living illustrate a **fourth** and closely related meaning of discipline—discipline as practices that maintain one in holy living. The Disciplines outlined such practices. So also did Wesley's independently published "Rules of the Band Societies" and "The Nature, Design, and General Rules of the United Societies."[18] These guided Methodists in the conduct of their interior lives of prayer, fasting, and Bible-reading; in relations with family and neighbors; in ministries to the poor, sick, and bereaved; in deportment and dress; in patterns of diligence, frugality, and self-denial; in attending to "all the ordinances of God"; in communal confession and forgiveness; in receiving criticism openly; and in leading a life of love. Wesley provided very specific guidelines under three headings for those whose desire to flee the wrath to come manifested itself in fruits of the Spirit. They would "evidence their desire of salvation,

> *First,* By doing no harm, by avoiding evil in every kind. . . .
>
> *Secondly,* By doing good. . . .
>
> *Thirdly,* By attending upon all the ordinances of God."[19]

The *Discipline* currently cites these Wesleyan imperatives with the prefatory note:

No motif in the Wesleyan tradition has been more constant than the link between Christian doctrine and Christian living. Methodists have always been strictly enjoined to maintain the unity of faith and good works through the means of grace, as seen in John Wesley's *The Nature, Design, and General Rules of the United Societies* (1743). The coherence of faith with ministries of love forms the discipline of Wesleyan spirituality and Christian discipleship.[20]

The Talbert vignette documents, in a variety of ways, how Methodist practice of holy living has changed and how actual practice *and* disciplined living can conflict with the letter of the *Discipline* and invite an exercise of discipline (the first four meanings in complex tension). Ellie Charlton and Jeanne Barnett invited the church's blessing on the informal covenant within which they sought to practice the faith (fourth meaning). However, that blessing contravened the rule or discipline under which clergy function (third meaning), in the *Discipline* (first meaning) and entailed juridical proceedings (third meaning).[21] Such blessings were, as Talbert indicates, proscribed within the Social Principles of the *Discipline*. There was some irony that initially the *Discipline* proscribed covenants within which homosexuals might live together in greater faithfulness in that section that most fully spells out the practices for Christian living today, namely the Social Principles. There the church has located its most explicit counsel on how United Methodists today, individually and corporately, ought to practice their faith.

A **fifth** aspect of discipline, in fact, points toward covenantal living as a Christian norm. This aspect perhaps can be more readily grasped from the Charles Wesley hymn. The practices of discipline, outlined in the General Rules and in the *Discipline* and referenced throughout the Wesleys' writings, bound Methodists together in systems of mutual accountability.

> Join we then our hearts and hands,
> Each to love provoke his friend;
> Run the way of his commands,
> And keep it to the end.

What Charles exhorts lyrically, he also proclaims as graciously already given: "Who of twain hath made us one, / Maintains our unity" the hymn promises. Discipline in class meeting, in the family, among friends, within the orders of ministry demands mutuality, community, covenant.

Following the Wesleyan imperative and claiming the promise of grace, Methodists have resisted bifurcating personal and social holiness. This commitment now finds expression in our "Social Principles," to which Talbert pays considerable attention in his decision. Congregations express their adherence to those principles on Sunday mornings in the Social Creed, an important Methodist contribution to ecumenical liturgical witness for a century. Since 1968, United Methodists have had access to denominational stances on social and personal holiness in the quadrennially published *Book of Resolutions of The United Methodist Church.* The 1968 edition, 96 pages in length, began with several timely statements on Vietnam and race, and concluded with a study document on "The Church and Family." The 2000 version runs to 863 pages requiring a long index, an elaborate table of contents, and thematic arrangement to provide access to the church's efforts to guide the faithful on social and personal ethics. One can hear echoes in the many pieces and sections of the church's long struggles over race and ethnicity, of its signal witness against alcoholism, of its courageous stands on war and peace, of its growing concern over the global human family, of its willingness to engage other living religions, of its self-critique, of its initiatives on women, of its concern for persons with handicapping conditions, and of its quandaries on sexual orientation. One could wish that *The Book of Resolutions* found its way into more United Methodist homes. Greater access might have made Bishop Talbert's agonies more readily shared.

A **sixth** meaning Bishop Talbert himself illustrates. He is "under discipline" and therefore accountable. He is not his own person. As a bishop of the church he upholds a rule and ruling with which he disagrees. He complies, in this case, against his own convictions and better judgment— because of his loyalty to the first four meanings of discipline, because of his covenantal bonds to the Council of Bishops, because of his sense of the obligations in the episcopal office, because of the rulings of the Judicial Council. Being under discipline, Talbert does not function on his own authority. The same holds for United Methodists generally and especially for United Methodist ministers. The minister is not on one's own. The minister is sent.[22]

However, one's sense of being sent can be conflicted, complex, in turmoil. To whom or what does one have highest loyalty? To one's own conscience, to the denomination, to the church universal, to God? And how does one recognize in a particular conviction who or what speaks?

Such quandaries point to a **seventh** meaning of discipline, discipline as fidelity to the gospel. Again, Talbert's statement nicely illustrates the meaning. He issues a prophetic critique of the *Discipline*, the Judicial Council, and the reigning policy in the church. He insists that blessings belong to God and that clergy do them under divine command. He speaks, on behalf of the gospel as he understands it, against the church's rules, an interpretation, of course, which would not be uniformly shared—his own prophetic utterance.[23] Discipline as the rule of God, as he grasps it, stands in judgment on *Discipline* as the rule of the denomination. To discipline the church in this fashion courts the hostile, repressive, destructive reaction always meted out to prophets. Methodists have had many such prophets and not infrequently dealt with them accordingly.[24] Discipline involves then the exercise of the teaching office, including instruction, judgment, chastisement, and reproof. Bishops rightly play such roles, but discipline in this judging sense belongs to the whole people of God and once was the special charge of class leaders. Discipline is exercised on the church as well as by the church. In the end, after all, discipline and judgment belong to God.

An **eighth** meaning is closely related, discipline as the good order of the church. Discipline, United Methodists hold, constitutes one of the defining task or "marks" of the church.[25] The church exists, can be discerned, is established, is marked where the word is truly preached, the sacraments rightly administered, and Christ's discipline exercised. The Confession of Faith of the Evangelical United Brethren Church defines the church as

> the redemptive fellowship in which the Word of God is preached by men divinely called, and the sacraments are duly administered according to Christ's own appointment. Under the discipline of the Holy Spirit the Church exists for the maintenance of worship, the edification of believers and the redemption of the world.[26]

And in the Methodist tradition, elders were ordained, from the days of Wesley, with language drawn from the Anglican Reformation "to minister the doctrine and Sacraments, and the discipline of Christ, as the Lord hath commanded."[27] In 1940, the Methodist Church amended the historic language to read: "to minister the doctrine of Christ, the Sacraments, and the discipline of the Church," phrasing continued through to the 1968 union.[28]

More recently the preferred formulation has been Word, Order, and Sacrament, and it recurs now through United Methodist *Disciplines*, particularly in the sections outlining ministry. For instance, the 1992 *Book of*

Discipline and *The United Methodist Book of Worship* speak of ordination as "a public act of the Church which indicates acceptance by an individual of God's call to the upbuilding of the Church through the ministry of Word, Sacrament, and Order and acknowledgment and authentication of this call by the Christian community through prayers and the laying on of hands."[29]

We should note that the 1996 General Conference added to the historical marks or defining tasks of the church, to the threefold definition that Methodists have long shared with Anglicans and also with the Reformed tradition, to the threefold office traditionally ascribed to Christ (prophet, priest, king). Now the formula reads: Service, Word, Sacrament, and Order. *The Book of Discipline* currently speaks of ordination as "fulfilled in leadership of the people of God through ministries of Service, Word, Sacrament, and Order." And new sections on "Servant Ministry and Servant Leadership," "Servant Ministry," and "Servant Leadership" begin the case for this new "mark" as shaped by ministry, message, and mission of Jesus.[30] Throughout the formula "Service, Word, Sacrament, and Order" replaces the classical threefold pattern.

The additional word "service" and replacement with a fourfold of the traditional threefold formula that echoes the offices of Christ requires, in my judgment, more in the way of biblical and theological rationale than the *Discipline* currently provides. More development of Christ's servanthood will not suffice. The exposition should attend to the whole formula and the relation of the ecclesial and christological offices. It should reflect, in particular, on the implications on our understanding of order and of the royal office of Christ by our removal there from of an important dimension of Christ's kingship and our order, namely service. Here, as in a number of changes to its polity or ministry, Methodism has undertaken an interesting innovation and now needs, in the interest of relations with the rest of the Christian church, to subject its reform to testing in good quadrilateral fashion.

At any rate, the new formula draws attention to itself and therefore to the import of the other items, including order, as marks of the church. All four or all three of Christ's offices come to focus and are exercised in superintendency, in episcopacy. To the bishops, in particular, belongs the responsibility of good order. "Those who superintend," the *Discipline* declares, "carry primary responsibility for ordering the life of the Church" and "are set apart for a ministry of general oversight and supervision."[31] These simple declarations will perhaps suffice here to underscore the point that Methodism takes discipline/order so seriously as to consecrate a special office for it, indeed two offices. Both bishops and district superintendents have responsibility for the discipline, for the good order of the church. And bishops report, unhappily, that discipline, particularly the disciplining of clergy, consumes more and more of their time and energy.[32]

Discipline in this sense as constitutive of the church and its governance was a point that Wesley shared with Calvin, though the former had, if anything, a richer and more nuanced sense thereof. Calvin affirmed, "Discipline depends for the most part on the power of the keys and upon spiritual jurisdiction." And he continued,

> [A]s the saving doctrine of Christ is the soul of the church, so does discipline serve as its sinews, through which the members of the body hold together, each in its own place. Therefore, all who desire to remove discipline or to hinder its restoration—whether they do this deliberately or out of ignorance—are surely contributing to the ultimate dissolution of the church.[33]

A **ninth** point summarizes the previous eight. It is that United Methodism understands discipline or order to be necessary and ingredient to the polity, procedure, structure, practice, mission, operation, ministry, and governance of the Church.[34] The church must be disciplined and disciplining. There is, further, a particularly Methodist and United Methodist way of being disciplined and disciplining. Its style or pattern differs from that of the Presbyterian or Reformed tradition that understands discipline and the church to constitute a series of courts. Methodists rather understand the church to be a series of superintended conversations about the Christian life. So, under the guidance of superintendents, the church "conferences" and "connections" (connects itself) into and under and for discipline/*Discipline*.[35] Conference writes the *Discipline*. Superintendents exercise discipline. Discipline is the overarching reality. Discipline is a way of daily life. Discipline is Methodist law. Discipline is its good news about fulfilling law. Discipline is outside the self. Discipline is the self.

What then is discipline? For United Methodists, it is a book, an exercise of ecclesiastical judgment, a way of living, a set of practices, loving mutuality in oversight, a recognized accountability, the state or act of being faithful to the gospel, the good order of the church, and the polity or governance of the church. Discipline functions as noun, verb, adverb, adjective. For Methodists, discipline constitutes the way of being Christian, of being church.

Issues

Commenting on recent United Methodist *Disciplines*, my colleague Thomas Frank notes several recent shifts—notably from structures that discipline to functions, from discipline to disciple-making, and from prescribed functional order to discretionary organization (polity).[36] In fact, as we have already remarked, shifts in the understanding of and challenges to the exercise of discipline have been ongoing for some time. Indeed, Wesley himself had to exhort his preachers frequently to "be exact in every branch of discipline."[37] He wrote one to put a wayward class leader out of "our Society," affirming, "If twenty of his class will leave the Society too, they must. The first loss is the best. Better forty members should be lost than our discipline lost. They are no Methodist that will bear no restraints."[38]

Has Wesley's discipline been largely lost—not only through the recent shifts that Frank documents but also in the senses that Wesley here meant it? Has it been lost in terms of the rich and clustered meanings that we outlined above—a book, an exercise of ecclesiastical judgment, a way of living, a set of practices, loving mutuality in oversight, a recognized accountability, the state or act of being faithful to the gospel, the good order of the church, and the polity or governance of the church?

To put the matter differently, have not the various meanings, expectations, duties, and structures been largely dissociated from one another? We list, after all, activities or concerns that do continue, in one form or another, as the exegesis of the Talbert statement demonstrates. But do we not tend, in fact, to identify each as a distinct responsibility, dissociate them readily from one another, and move them easily under different labels than "discipline"? For instance, terms like spirituality, formation, accountability, law, integrity, and polity would be more typically applied to exercises that we discern in the Talbert vignette and gather under "discipline." And do we not tend, when we identify disciple-making as the embracive task of the church, to lose its richer nuances, to lose the explanatory sentences that follow in ¶ 201,[39] for instance, and to equate discipling with recruitment?[40]

The Wesleys were clear that discipline made the Christian and constituted the church. John several times affirmed, as he did in a letter to Adam Clarke, "It is a true saying, 'The soul and the body make the man, and the spirit and discipline make a Christian.'"[41] The rich, clustered meanings of discipline echo through the refrains of the hymn of Charles with which we began this chapter. And John gathered the nuances together in his sermon "On God's Vineyard," where he affirmed:

> It is certain that in this respect the Methodists are a highly favoured people. Nothing can be more simple, nothing more rational, than the Methodist discipline: it is entirely founded on common sense, particularly applying the general rules of Scripture. Any person determined to save his soul may be united (this is the only condition required) with them. But this desire must be evidenced by three marks: avoiding all known sin, doing good after his power, and attending all the ordinances of God. He is then placed in such a class as is convenient for him, where he spends about an hour in a week. And the next quarter, if nothing is objected to him, he is admitted into the Society. And therein he may continue as long as he continues to meet his brethren and walks according to his profession.

After describing the Methodist services, Wesley continued:

> On Sunday evening the Society meets; but care is taken to dismiss them early, that all the heads of families may have time to instruct their several households. Once a quarter the principal preacher in every circuit examines every member of the societies therein. By this means, if the behaviour of anyone is blameable, which is frequently to be expected in so numerous a body of people, it is easily discovered, and either the offence or the offender removed in time.[42]

Similarly, in his sermon on "The Late Work of God in North America," Wesley identified the fatal defect in the evangelistic ministry of George Whitefield, the lack of discipline:

> [I]t was a true saying, which was common in the ancient church, 'The soul and the body make a man, and the spirit and discipline make a Christian.' But those who were more or less affected by Mr. Whitefield's preaching had no discipline at all. They had no shadow of discipline; nothing of the kind. They were formed into no societies. They had no Christian connection with each other, nor were ever taught to watch over each others' souls. So that if any fell into lukewarmness, or even into sin, he had none to lift him up. . . .[43]

The deterioration in Methodist discipline has been ongoing, perhaps as Wesley's statement indicates, from the very start. Throughout the nineteenth century preachers and people registered complaints about the loss of discipline. Often they located the symbol of decline in the disuse of the class meeting. In the twentieth century Methodist discipline came more to be symbolized by the prohibitions against drinking and smoking. Queries on those two constituted the centerpiece of my ordination examination, playing a far more important role than Wesley's "Historic Examination" or worries over my understanding of the evangelical doctrines.[44] The oversimplification of discipline, by focusing the whole of doctrine and discipline around drink or, as now, around matters of sexual orientation, may itself contribute to the loss of the richer and the clustering of meanings thereof.

Oversimplification has occurred as well because of the way Methodists (with other Christians shaped by Pietism or Evangelicalism) make ministers into moral surrogates or scapegoats, expecting them to live by and thereby symbolize the commitment of the community as a whole to ethical norms. By not smoking or drinking the minister stood for the rich, complex array of disciplines and forms of piety that Methodism had evolved. Similarly today, the community expects ministers to symbolize its adherence to norms on sexuality and marriage, both in their person and in the rituals they perform.

Expectations of high ethical standards for clergy are, of course, entirely appropriate, as Dennis Campbell shows in his discussion of the representational nature of ministry.[45] And the huge numbers of incidents of clergy misconduct, especially sexual misconduct, indicate that the clergy, individually and as a covenanted community, have failed the church grievously. Bishops and district superintendents report, for instance, that they expend inordinate proportions of their time to ministerial misconduct. To this matter, to sin and moral failure in ministry, Will Willimon devotes major sections of his book, *Pastor*.[46]

However, having ministers live by the norms and disciplines of the Christian life should not absolve the whole people of God from these fundamental baptismal expectations *nor* absolve ministers from their pastoral administration of discipline. Thomas Oden rightly complained that though the long tradition of pastoral counsel prescribed "The Work of the Holy Spirit in Comfort, Admonition, and Discipline," "yet it is conspicuously absent in modern pastoral writings."[47] Oden devotes a chapter to *nouthesia*, the admonition, counsel, reproof, instruction and modeling that he links closely with teaching and terms a "central pastoral duty."[48] In good Wesleyan fashion, Oden connects disciplining and teaching with sanctification. In the Spirit, individuals, ministers, and community discipline others and discipline themselves toward "penitence, purification, pardon, reformation and restitution."[49] And within this discussion of ecclesial and pastoral disciplining, Oden treats expectations of ministerial conduct. There he suggests that the ministry has not been well served by its embrace of professionalism and reduction of its norms and high expectations into "feeble" professional ethics.

The translation of ministerial discipline into professional ethics on which Oden comments may be part of a larger pattern. Methodism does seem to have contributed materially to the field of ethics, producing from its ranks a number of important ethicists, in part, perhaps the long legacy of Boston Personalism. And one might posit that ethical treatises, particularly those conceived or aimed broadly, do sustain much of the tradition's concern for discipline, disciplining, and the disciplined life.[50] But can ethics, even at the hand of Methodist ethicists, sustain all that Wesleyans have meant by discipline, and can ethics function with discipline's embracive mandates? Will it, can it, speak for Christian formation, for growth in spirituality (holiness), for mutuality in oversight (covenant groups), and for the whole structure of corporate Christian life (polity)? If not, ethical guidance will need to be augmented by these larger dimensions of discipline.

Christians as well as Jews have also insisted, from biblical times onward, that discipline or *paidea* belongs also to parents. Israel and the church have understood parental and pastoral roles of training and of discipline to be inseparable and to be human duties under God's judging and redemptive hand.[51] The shepherding role, to reiterate, belongs to the whole people of God, not just to the clergy. The *Discipline* offers much in the way of guidance to the whole flock, but it does so without making that guidance genuine disciplines for the people. The church locates Mr. Wesley's "General Rules" among our "Standards," but most United Methodists, I suspect, would view them as historical documents. On the other hand, the guidance for Christian living in the present takes pertinent and expressive form in Part IV, "Social Principles" and in the "Social Creed." Neither the former as ethical ideals nor the latter as a confession of principles sets out disciplines for the whole people of God. The Baptismal service and the paragraphs on "The Meaning of Membership" (¶ 216-20) come closer to the Wesleyan pattern, but focus really on discipleship, address discipline in relation to the church, and exhort rather than prescribe. Members as well as clergy have to work to grasp the richness of Wesleyan discipline in the *Discipline*.

Understanding Discipline Scripturally

Methodists read the Bible into their practices of discipline and read their discipline out of the Bible, a pattern that we can claim for each of the "marks," those examined here and the longer listing. Methodists understand discipline scripturally in a different fashion than those in the Reformed or Calvinist tradition. The Reformed—think, for instance, of the Puritans—intended, when they spoke of "discipline out of the Word," that churchly forms and activities should be literally and precisely those of the first century. They wanted the structure or form of the church in their day to track what they found in Acts. They wanted doctrine to be that found in Romans and other letters of Paul. They wanted to exercise discipline after the manner of the Pastorals. So Puritans founded congregations of the Word led by elders and deacons, preached election in Christ and through the Spirit, and disciplined with an eye to the law given in Moses as affirmed by Jesus.

Methodists have been no less steeped in the Word. If I understand us aright, we have made discipline, disciplining, disciplined our noun, verb, adverb, and adjective by keeping our eye on the scripturally given purpose or *telos* of discipline. We have not sought, in the main, to replicate the precise form or limit ourselves to the activity of the first century. Indeed, we remember and celebrate John Wesley's creativity in borrowing structures and processes from the long Christian tradition and the best and most redemptive processes of his day. Following Wesley we feel comfortable in reading the whole Bible for its inspiration of life today. However, we take particularly to heart, as did he, the passages that speak of discipleship, of following Christ, of living according to the divine Will, of life shaped by the Spirit—in short of what we term the evangelical doctrines.

So we take guidance in reading the whole Bible from passages like 1 Peter 1:13-25, which begins:

> Therefore prepare your minds for action; discipline yourselves; set all your hope on the grace that Jesus Christ will bring you when he is revealed. Like obedient children, do not be conformed to the desires that you formerly had ignorance. Instead, as he who called you is holy, be holy yourselves, in all your conduct; for it is written, "You shall be holy, for I am holy."

With such guidance from 1 Peter, we do indeed attend in the whole Bible to those laws, those commandments, those expectations enunciated by or reaffirmed in Christ. The disciplined life, for individual and community, is to be a holy life. So we can sing with Charles:

> O that all with us might prove
> The fellowship of saints!
> Find supplied, in Jesus' love,
> What every member wants:
> Grasp we our high calling's prize,
> Feel our sins on earth forgiven,
> Rise, in his whole image rise,
> And meet our Head in heaven!

Conclusion

The rich and clustered meanings of discipline one may find laid out in, but diffused through, the *Discipline* in its complicated sections and protocols on "The Ministry of the Ordained," chapter 2 of Part V. Read carefully—

- the discussion of the meaning of ordination and conference membership,
- the introspection and mutual testing in candidacy,
- the expectations for diaconal and presbyteral orders,
- the processes for commissioning,
- the serious and probing questions for written and oral examination on both commissioning and ordination levels,
- the "Historic Examination" questions for both orders, and
- the protocols in professional or clergy ethics—

read carefully; those discussions yield an adequate overall understanding of discipline. Those eighty or more pages frame the roles and expectations for the several offices of ministry so as to put the dimensions of discipline for clergy together into a single chapter.

The same point can be made about the *Discipline* as a whole. Our "discipline" for the people called Methodist is there. But we have diffused it through a huge and sprawling volume of nearly 800 pages. I rather suspect that many if not most persons encountering the *Discipline* or experiencing its policies would not gather those expectations, processes, and forms together under the word "discipline." Or, if they did, it would be because they were all to be found in the book, in the *Discipline*. The suspicion with which I began this chapter remains. Few United Methodists, I fear, can find "discipline" adequately and fully developed in the *Discipline*.

And yet United Methodists do sustain, albeit under different labels and without grasping their connection, the various activities and forms—the nouns, verbs, adverbs, and adjectives—that might be gathered under discipline, disciplining, disciplined. Perhaps they need a word for it.

CHAPTER FOUR

Catholic

1 HAPPY the souls to Jesus joined,[1]
And saved by grace alone,
Walking in all his ways they find
Their heaven on earth begun.

2 The church triumphant in thy love,
Their mighty joys we know;
They sing the Lamb in hymns above,
And we in hymns below.

3 Thee in thy glorious realm they praise,
And bow before thy throne,
We in the kingdom of thy grace:
The kingdoms are but one.

4 The holy to the holiest leads,
From thence our spirits rise,
And he that in thy statutes treads
Shall meet thee in the skies.

When United Methodists recite the Apostles' or Nicene Creeds and come to declare the church as "catholic," they are invited by an asterisk to an alternative affirmation, "universal." Ambivalence about the term "catholic" and about catholicity by no means confines itself to the creeds. On the one hand, United Methodism can be counted on for almost any unitive effort, any cooperative endeavor, any life and work enterprise. From the beginning of the ecumenical movement, Methodists assumed leadership, as they do today. Methodist money kept and keeps ecumenism in business. And United Methodism has given official consent to or affirmation of the important unitive initiatives, as we will note below. On the other hand, most Methodists remain ignorant of official commitments and indifferent to organizations and programs that work toward unity. The rank and file, by and large, do not know the work of the cadre of Methodist ecumenists or the commitments made by them on our behalf. A more serious gap exists on ecumenism and catholicity between the church's leadership, on the one side, and its clergy and lay members, on the other, than on virtually any other United Methodist commitment. Yet, catholicity constitutes one of the "marks" of Methodism.

The "catholic spirit," a consistent thread in the verse of Charles and in the theology and preaching of John Wesley,[2] both the Wesleys understood as founded on the common witness of the orthodox heritage, unity in essentials, an orientation toward common mission, a disciplined life, and bonds of love. Wesley affirmed in the sermon "Catholic Spirit":

> "If thine heart is as my heart," if thou lovest God and all mankind, I ask no more: "Give me thine hand."
>
> I mean, first, love me. . . . Love me with a very tender affection, as a friend that is closer than a brother; as a brother in Christ, a fellow-citizen of the new Jerusalem, a fellow-soldier engaged in the same warfare, under the same captain of our salvation.
>
> I mean, secondly, commend me to God in all thy prayers; . . . Pray that the love of God and of all mankind may be more largely poured into my heart; . . .
>
> I mean, thirdly, provoke me to love and to good works.
>
> I mean, lastly, love me not in word only, but in deed and in truth. So far as in conscience thou canst (retaining still thy own opinions and thy own manner of worshipping God), join with me in the work of God, and let us go on hand in hand.[3]

This catholic spirit American Methodists have lived out. They seldom equaled Wesley's level of precision in its articulation. And against its mandates and ideals they experienced constant temptations and challenges. The competitiveness and acrimony of a denominational society rewarded active self-promotion, clarity about one's confessional distinctives, and a combative religious free enterprise. Efforts to Christianize American society might temporarily occasion common mission and reinforce the catholic spirit only to wreck on some matter of policy or principle. Real differences among Christians on language, race, ethnicity, class, region found expression in religious as well as political conflict. In the new nation, with its experiment of religious freedom and separation of church and state, the religious story was one of division. And Methodism itself suffered division after division. Still one can say that Methodists labored *for* Christian unity and labored *in* Christian unity.

We might illustrate American Methodism's catholic spirit with any number of incidents or persons, at any period in our history, of course including the twentieth century when Methodists played key ecumenical roles. One can see it as well in our early history, as the life and work of Bishop Christian Newcomer, successor to William Otterbein among the United Brethren, vividly illustrates. Christian Newcomer explored Christian unity in breaking bread, in conference, on the road, in common witness, in ordinations, through dialogue, and in proposals for merger.

Vignette

Vignette[Lancaster County, PA] [August 1813]

21st—Today a sacramental meeting commenced at Peter Seitz's, I spoke first, from Psalm 130, v. 7; at night I preached again from Psalm 40, v. 2, 3, 4.

Sunday 22d—An uncommonly large congregation had this day collected; I preached with great liberty from 1st Peter 5, v. 5 to 9. I was followed by a brother in the English language; a vast number came to the Lord's table, and we had a melting time. At night I preached again at John Buck's; here we again had a soul-reviving meeting; nearly every person present melted into tears; some cried for mercy, others shouted and praised God. 23d—This forenoon we held our Love-feast; we had truly a day of Pentecost: all the glory be to our God. I lodged with Rodebach . . . . 26th— This forenoon the session of our Conference commenced; upwards of twenty preachers were present; poor unworthy me was elected their president. The Conference continued until the 28th; all things were done in brotherly love, and the greatest unanimity prevailed throughout the sessions: bless the Lord, O my soul! for all his mercy. The Conference was concluded, and I rode 11 miles yet to Jacob Hautz's. . . .

[Ohio]

September 1—This evening I reached Steubenville; . . . 2d—The Ohio Conference is here in session. I went this morning to pay a visit to Bishop Asbury, who is present; he lodges with Mr. Wells, where we took breakfast together; I went with him to Conference, and delivered a communication from our Conference. Here I found several brethren to whom I was known; was cordially invited to lodge at Br. Noland's, during my stay, which invitation I cheerfully accepted.

Sunday 5th—Bishops Asbury and McKendree both preached to-day to a congregation estimated at more than 2000 persons. 6th—This forenoon I received a communication from the Conference to the Brethren in our next Conference which is to assemble in Montgomery county, Ohio. After taking an affectionate farewell of the two Bishops and the other Brethren, I dined once more with my kind host Br. Wm. Noland; commended him and his amiable family to God in prayer, and set out at three o'clock in the afternoon; crossed the Ohio river, and staid for the night in a little village. . . .

[Pennsylvania]
11th—This day a Sacramental meeting commenced in Mount Pleasant; I spoke first, from Psalm 40, v. 6; Br. Fechtig followed me. At night I preached in Bonnet's school-house, from Acts 16, v. 30, 31, and lodged at Worman's.

Sunday 12th—This forenoon Christian Berger spoke first, then Jacob Winter. I preached again, from John 3, v. 6, 7; lodged with Sloderbeck. 13th—This forenoon we held our Love-feast; . . .

[Maryland]
October 1st—This morning we came to Baltimore; old father Otterbein is very weak and feeble in body, but strong and vigorous in spirit, and full of hope of a blissful immortality and eternal life. He was greatly rejoiced at our arrival, informed me that he had received a letter from the Brethren in the west, wherein he was requested to ordain me, by the laying on of hands, to the office of elder and preacher of the gospel, before his departure: adding, "I have always considered myself too unworthy to perform this solemn injunction of the Apostle, but now I perceived the necessity of doing so, before I shall be removed." He then requested to know whether I had any objection to make, and if not whether the present would not be a suitable time. I replied, that I firmly believed solemn ordination to the ministry had been enjoined and practiced by the Apostles; . . . 2d—This forenoon the Vestry and several other members of the church, assembled at the house of father Otterbein. The old man addressed us in so spiritual and powerful a manner, that all behold him with astonishment. It appeared as if he had received particular unction from above, to perform this solemn act. After addressing a throne of grace with great fervency for a blessing, he called on Br. Wm. Ryland, an Elder of the Methodist Episcopal church, (who had been invited for the purpose,) to assist him in the ordination; we were accordingly ordained to the office of Elders in the ministry, by the laying on of hands. John Hildt, a member of the Vestry, had been appointed Secretary. He executed certificates of Ordination to each of us, in the German and English languages. Which certificates were then signed by

father William Otterbein and delivered to each of us. At night we preached in the church; I lodged with Otterbein.

Sunday 3d—This forenoon Br. Hoffman preached first, I followed him; Br. Shaffer assisted in the administration of the Lord's Supper. A great many persons came to the table of the Lord with contrite hearts and streaming eyes; this was truly a day of grace to many souls: unto God be all the glory. . . .

Sunday 10th—We had a Sacramental meeting at Shauman's church; Hoffman and John Sneider rode home with me, where we had a blessed meeting by candle-light. 16th, and

Sunday 17th—We had a Sacramental meeting at Leonard Middlekauff's; at night we had a blessed meeting at Henry Kumler's. Several were in great distress, and some obtained peace with God in the pardon of their sins. . . .

[Pennsylvania]

10th—This forenoon we had meeting at John Walter's; at night I preached at Mr. Mack's, near New Berlin, from Psalm 34, last four verses. 11th—This purpose of our journey to this place was to try whether a union could not be effected between the society of the United Brethren in Christ, and the people denominated the Albright Brethren. This forenoon the following Brethren were present, viz: Chr. Crum, Joseph Hoffman, Jacob Bowlus and myself of our society; and Miller, Walter, Dreisbach and Niebel, of the Albright Brethren. Our consultation continued until the 13th, but we were not able to effect a union. The greatest stumbling block appeared to be this, that according to our discipline our local preachers have a vote in the Conference as well as the travelling preachers; this was a sine qua non which the Albright Brethren could or would not accede to; so we parted and came at night to Youngman'stown where we lodged.

. . . .

[Maryland]

17th—I rode in company with Jacob Bowlus; we staid for the night at a public house 21 miles from Baltimore. 18th—We arrived in the city; the Methodist Conference is in session here. 19th—We attended the Conference and delivered a communication from our Conference.

Sunday 20th—This forenoon Jacob Gruber preached in Otterbein's church; in the afternoon, Jacob Bowlus; I spoke at night. . . . 23d This day the Conference came to a close; in the forenoon Bishop Asbury preached a funeral discourse for the late Wm. Otterbein, from Revelation 3, v. 10, 11. The congregation was so numerous, that the church was much too small to contain all the people. Here were ministers of different persuasions assembled to pay the last tribute of respect to this servant of the Most High; Methodists, United Brethren, Lutherans, Presbyterians, and Episcopalians,—all mingled together to pay homage to departed worth. Bishop McKendree closed the service with fervent prayer. . . .

Sunday [April] 3d—I attended a meeting of the Albright Brethren. . . .

Sunday 10th—I attended meeting with the River Brethren. . . .

[May] 24th—This day our Conference commenced in Hagers-town, and continued until the 27th. More preachers were present than at any Conference before. The Brethren elected poor unworthy Christian Newcomer as Bishop and Superintendent, for three years. May God have mercy on me, and grant me his assisting grace to discharge my duty faithfully. 28th and Sunday, 29th—We had a Sacramental meeting at the Antietam. . . .[4]

Commentary

The early American Methodists, United Brethren, and Evangelicals may not have been terribly good at theologizing about catholicity or in verbalizing their hope for the great hope of unity in Christ. However, their actions and daily regiments attested a *very* catholic spirit. What they lacked in formal doctrine they more than compensated for in gesture, as one can see in these 1813–14 selections from the journal of Bishop Christian Newcomer, successor to William Otterbein as leader of the United Brethren. Across denominational, linguistic, and racial lines, Newcomer in particular and Methodists more generally broke bread, met in conference, traveled together, bore common witness (especially in time of grief), shared in ordinations, carried on dialogue, and made formal efforts at unity.

First, United Brethren, Methodists, and Evangelicals broke bread together. Three meals epitomized the several modalities of unity. One bound together those within the household of faith. Two other meals united Methodists with those beyond their membership. Love feasts stylized patterns of close affectionate unity that existed on the many occasions when United Brethren, Evangelicals, and Methodists gathered as Christian family. Love feasts united members, those jointly fleeing together the wrath to come. Through witness, scripture, singing, prayer, and offerings Methodists found unity over a simple meal of bread and water. Attendance by strangers was restricted by *Disciplinary* (Wesleyan) precept. This meal united those within the Methodist family. But many love feasts occurred at quarterly meetings, which drew large crowds and functioned evangelistically. In such public settings the love feast's intimacy would have been readily perceived, its impact on participants envied, and its special purpose the more remarkable. So this meal that bound together the family of faith drew wider attention to the special, "Pentecostal," affectionate unity experienced within.

On many of these same quarterly meeting or camp meeting occasions, Methodists opened a second meal, the Lord's Table, that is the communion table, to "vast numbers," welcomed the tears, cries of mercy, and shouts of praise, and celebrated the fact that many communed. Just how open Methodists ought to keep our table remains a contentious issue. Absent the effectively used and frequently celebrated love feasts of the early nineteenth century, some today would cherish the presuppositions and expectations that Methodists had once held for their special meal for the common Christian Eucharist. Others want a genuinely open table, presuming the Lord's Supper to be available even to the non-baptized and to be a converting ordinance. Both sides in this debate appeal to John Wesley. Early Methodists had the luxury of other meals than communion in terms of which to enact their unity within and their participation in the wider unity in Christ. In addition to communion as a feast for the baptized and love feast as meal for the path to holiness, Methodists had yet a third more common meal.

Early United Brethren, Methodists, and Evangelicals shared common meals on the road, around the campfire, or in the homes where they bedded for the night, sometimes eucharistically with "brethren" and "sisters," sometimes evangelistically or apologetically with families outside the faith. The breakfast that Newcomer ate with Francis Asbury and the "affectionate farewell" bid Asbury, William McKendree, and the other Methodist brethren resembled the more daily sharing of meal, praying with a family, and blessing them on departure. Itinerants routinely broke bread where they stayed for the night, seizing such openings, when possible, as evangelistic opportunities.

Meals—love feast, Lord's Supper, and what would now be known as dinner on the grounds—marked out respectively the nurturing unity experienced within class and society, the resurrection unity shared with Christians generally, and the unity of all humanity, indeed the whole creation.[5] Only the second of these we would deem properly sacramental.

And it is worth underscoring the great importance of the "sacramental meetings" to Newcomer and the United Brethren. However, there was something of a sacramental quality to the other two meals. Or to put it another way, the early Brethren and Methodists encountered one another and offered the world a gospel most dramatically expressed in the sacrament. In the sacrament they grasped something of the unity that Christ offered to the world and affirmed the shared doctrinal heritage to which the sacrament pointed. And that evangelistic unitive gesture, further nurtured in the intimacy of love feast, gave even the common meal a sacramental and gracious quality.

Our other points build on this first. **Second,** the unity and catholicity that the several meals ritualized, Methodist, United Brethren and Evangelical conferences choreographed in social and dramatic fashion. The "brotherly love" and "greatest unanimity"—this special, intense bonding within the fraternity of preachers—gave annual conferences a class- or band-like quality. The spiritual intensity of United Brethren conferences can be readily seen in their early Minutes, which routinely noted the class-like opening exercise: "Then each of the preachers spoke of his experience."[6]

The spiritual intimacy of conferences made them more, rather than less, invitational to the wider Methodist community, indeed the public more generally. When preachers convened, they performed. They preached. So conferences routinely functioned both with closed and intimate sessions and with open and evangelical sessions. Conferences, therefore, found ways to embrace the wider local community, two thousand of whom convened at an early Methodist Ohio conference. Similarly, conferences worked across denominational boundaries. UBC conferences welcomed an Asbury into a their gatherings. And a Newcomer found welcome in Methodist, Evangelical (Albright), and River Brethren meetings. Conferences had, then, their love-feast or class-like quality and an evangelistic and catholic openness.[7]

Third, out of and into conferences, quarterly meetings, and camp meetings early Methodists would ride with others—as the chapter on itinerancy demonstrates—a connectionalism of the road where long rides encouraged close unity among brothers (and sometimes sisters), exchange with other Christians, and opportunities for discourse with those outside the faith. Sometimes the companions of the road were Deists, as Colbert reported, or Baptists, as he noted elsewhere, and the conversation turned combative rather than catholic. On other occasions, a genuine community of the road occurred.

Fourth, early Methodists bore common witness, especially in time of grief, as did the MEC conference in the funeral for William Otterbein, at which Asbury preached and McKendree prayed, a service attended by Methodists, United Brethren, Lutherans, Presbyterians, and Episcopalians. Other crises, then as now, bound Christians together in common endeavor.

Fifth, the role of Otterbein in Asbury's ordination is well known, perhaps less so the deliberate effort by the United Brethren to achieve a similar ecumenical sign by the inclusion of Methodist Elder William Ryland in Otterbein's ordination of Newcomer. The symbolism of Newcomer's election to the episcopacy on Aldersgate Day was doubtless unintended.

Sixth, the United Brethren, Methodists, and Evangelicals carried on dialogue at various levels and through informal conversations and written overtures. The early Evangelical Association minutes attest such explorations, particularly those from the General Conference of 1816 for which unity dialogues with the United Brethren seem to be the primary item of business.[8]

Seventh, at several points those dialogues led to formal explorations of unity. In the selection above, Newcomer reported on the efforts made between the United Brethren and Albright Brethren. The disagreement over the role of local preachers, like Newcomer's sensitivity to apostolic practice and Otterbein's ordination by appropriate laying on of hands, indicate efforts to participate in the catholic faith and to orient catholicity by canons of orthodox belief and practice. Unity would not be achieved by mere warmheartedness. It would predicate agreement on essential doctrines. And it would be for mission, effective common witness, the transformation of the world.[9] A church made "one" and universal would also be holy and apostolic.

Issues: The Ideal and Present Commitments

In his gestures of unity—breaking bread, meeting in conference, traveling together, bearing common witness (especially in time of grief), sharing ordinations, carrying on dialogue, and making formal efforts at unity—Newcomer evidenced the several dimensions of Methodist catholicity. He anticipated important elements of what John Deschner, translating Wesley, identifies as the four elements of United Methodism's ecumenical policy, particularly the first three:

(1) the goal of "an inclusive church unity as a witness to God's way of healing and renewing the broken human community,"[10]

evidenced in the common meal, the quarterly and camp meetings opened to the world, and the conversations on the road with those outside the faith;

(2) a sign of integrity in "an inclusive, visible fellowship around the table in Holy Communion,"

> evidenced in the "open" Lord's Supper, the eucharistic meetings and meals between Asbury and Newcomer, the presence in the other denomination's conferences;

(3) the immediate step of "a full inclusive and mutual recognition of members and ministers,"

> evidenced in joint services, ordinations that involved leaders of other denominations, and on-going dialogue;

(4) the anticipation of fuller unity in "a future truly ecumenical conciliar event of witness."

> not achieved in the nineteenth century but evidenced in formal proposals for unity that these movements offered one another from time to time.

While these elements of policy all point ahead and indicate that The United Methodist Church has a distance to go in achieving its catholic and ecumenical ends, the churches have achieved some of what Newcomer sought and Wesley espoused. They have continued gestures and patterns like those exemplified by Newcomer that in a variety of ways expressed the catholic spirit and sought unity around the shared Christian doctrinal heritage. Most notably, the bodies for whose unification he personally labored—Methodist, United Brethren, Evangelical—did come together to form The United Methodist Church. And in that union the new church imbedded the catholic spirit, understanding the bringing together of traditions representing the major strands of the Protestant Reformation as pointing further ahead to still greater unity. That ecumenical, unitive, or catholic commitment has been imbedded in United Methodism—in its structure, policy, and program, indeed, in its very constitution—in

• the Preamble to the Constitution,[11] which situates the newly constituted church within the universal church;
• Article III of the Constitution, which incorporates Articles I and II of the Restrictive Rules that protect the Articles of Religion and the Confession of Faith, thereby drawing into a shared confessional deposit the theological witness of the Anglican, Reformed, Lutheran, and Anabaptist (Mennonite) heritages, defining the church in classic Reformation terms (Articles), and claiming its classic marks, "one, holy, apostolic and catholic" (Confession);

- Article IV of the Constitution on the "Inclusiveness of the Church," which proclaims The United Methodist Church "a part of the church universal" and commits it to overcoming all those forces and factors that divide the human family;
- Article V of the Constitution on "Ecumenical Relations," which affirms "as part of the church universal, The United Methodist Church believes the Lord of the church is calling Christians everywhere to strive toward unity."

The ecumenical, unitive, or catholic commitment, United Methodism also builds into its structure, policy, and program elsewhere in the *Discipline*—in

- "Our Doctrinal Heritage" in Part II, which locates United Methodism within the "the historic Christian faith" and the "common heritage with Christians of every age and nation," and sets out "Basic Christian Affirmations" that United Methodists confess with all Christians;
- the final affirmations, which include the following statements elaborating on the ground of and commitment to that unity:

  With other Christians, we declare the essential oneness of the church in Christ Jesus.

  Our avowed ecumenical commitment as United Methodists is to gather our own doctrinal emphases into the larger Christian unity, there to be made more meaningful in a richer whole.

  It is as Christians involved in ecumenical partnership that we embrace and examine our distinctive heritage.

- "Our Doctrinal History," which begins by insisting that the church's constitutive traditions "understood themselves as standing in the central stream of Christian spirituality and doctrine," characterizes the church's vocation as "catholic spirit," and concludes by positing the recovery, updating, and reinvigorating of "our distinctive doctrinal heritage"—catholic, evangelical, and reformed—as essential to both evangelism and ecumenical dialogue;
- "Our Theological Task," which ends with a section on "Ecumenical Commitment" insisting that "Christian unity is not an option" but is mandated theologically, biblically, and practically—"a gift to be received and expressed";

- "The Ministry of All Christians" in Part IV (1996), which situated important United Methodist rubrics—the journey of a connectional people, servant ministry, servant leadership, the call to inclusiveness, and the fulfillment of ministry through The United Methodist Church—within the narration of the longer and larger story of God's covenantal initiatives; though it must be conceded that this strongly ecumenical or catholic note has been muted in the 2000 *Discipline*, which retains the former overall titles "The Ministry of All Christians," "The Mission and Ministry of the Church," and "The Churches," but leads instead with a missional affirmation that locates that task in local churches and in disciple-making;[12]
- Part V, Chapter 1, "The Local Church," which in framing the church's global mission makes provision for cooperative parishes and ecumenical shared ministries;
- the section on "Church Membership," ¶ 214, which states (1996): "The United Methodist Church, a fellowship of believers, is as a church also an inherent part of the church universal . . ." and (2000): "The United Methodist Church is a part of the holy catholic (universal) church, as we confess in the Apostles' Creed." ¶ 215 (2000) affirms: "*The Wider Church*—A member of any local United Methodist church is a member of the denomination and the catholic (universal) church." The section on membership sets very inclusive standards and broad expectations for all the baptized (¶ 219);
- The Ministry of the Ordained (Chapter 2 of Part V), which frames the ministry of deacons and elders in terms of the ministry of Christ and of all Christians, understands its apostolic form, conceives the call as gift from God, and therefore places those ordained as "in covenant with all Christians, especially with those whom they lead and serve in ministry." Ordination, then, like baptism, we do on behalf of the whole church;
- the episcopal or superintending office, among whose tasks is "to seek and be a sign of the unity of the faith" and "to exercise the discipline of the whole Church" (¶ 404) and specifically "to provide liaison and leadership in the quest for Christian unity in ministry, mission, and structure and in the search for strengthened relationships with other living faith communities" (¶ 414);
- the General Commission on Christian Unity and Interreligious Concerns (GCCUIC), and its corresponding boards or officers on jurisdictional, conference, district, and congregational levels, charged explicitly to exercise "ecumenical leadership" toward Christian unity and dialogue with other faiths, cultures, and ideologies; and

• the several "Interdenominational Agencies"—World Methodist Council (WMC), Churches Uniting in Christ (previously the Consultation on Church Union or COCU), the National Council of Churches, the World Council of Churches, the Commission on Pan-Methodist Cooperation, and the American Bible Society—membership in which the *Discipline* explicitly acknowledges and leadership for which the *Discipline* charges to the bishops and GCCUIC leadership (¶ 2401).

United Methodism's formal commitments to unity and catholicity set impressive standards and directions and give the appearance of single-mindedness and coherence. In actual practice, various kinds of catholicities beckon the church in different directions, the genuine laborers for unity and catholicity remain few, the church at all levels voices more commitment than it proves willing to honor, some within the denomination express open hostility to ecumenical efforts, and many remain absolutely oblivious to investments long made.

Catholicity: Alternative Futures

As may be apparent in this long rehearsal, the church has committed itself to not one but several different schemes of catholicity. These may nicely cohere in the eschaton when all things are made one. Under the constraints of finitude, the several unitive or catholic possibilities presume different constellations of shared belief, pull in somewhat different directions and compete for the church's energies, imagination, and loyalty.[13] Each direction invites the church into a future catholicity of a distinct hue. A brief description of our several catholic options would seem in order.

Interreligious dialogue—particularly with representatives of Islam and Judaism, but also with those of Buddhism, Hinduism, Confucianism, and other world religions—represents the broadest form of catholicity, anticipated perhaps in the common meals that the Newcomers and Asburys ate with folk outside the Christian family. Such conversations have excited United Methodists at national levels, especially through the work of GCCUIC, whose name and charge embrace "Interreligious Concerns," and also have institutionalized themselves in locales around the country. By its "Social Principles," United Methodism commits to respect the "Rights of Religious Minorities."[14] More positively, General Conference has issued guidelines for interreligious conversations and relations.[15] Noteworthy as well are efforts by United Methodists in organizations and individually. For instance, Diana Eck,

United Methodist and director of "The Pluralism Project" at Harvard, by research, speeches, Web site, and CD-ROM documents the dramatic pluralism of North American society and has been especially influential on GCCUIC. Also worth remarking is United Methodist participation at local levels in joint ministries, missions, social service endeavors, and the like, which have comparable broad religious participation, sometimes achieved through keeping their focus on the tasks at hand.

United Methodism, through the World Methodist Council (WMC), participates in formal **bilateral dialogues** with Roman Catholics, Lutherans, the Reformed, Orthodoxy, and Anglicanism.[16] Into such dialogues have gone much of the creative theological energies of the several churches. United Methodists participate in the world dialogues alongside others in the Wesleyan family from across the globe, being driven in such conversation back to the foundations that Methodists share, that is, to the Wesleys. When United Methodists mount such dialogues on a denominational level they can bear witness out of their several confessional heritages—the holiness, disciplined, connectional, and Arminian practices of the Wesleys, William Otterbein, Martin Boehm, and Jacob Albright;[17] the continued resonances of Anglicanism, especially those liturgical; the confessional impulses from the Lutheran, Anabaptist, and Reformed heritages represented by Albright, Boehm, and Otterbein; and through all these the fullness of the catholic tradition, including especially the Eastern "fathers."[18] When undertaking bilaterals in the future on a denominational level, United Methodists may well need to particularize further and to allow for separate conversations in the church's distinctive national, linguistic, cultural, and political settings. The same point holds for several of the unitive options.

For United Methodism, especially, the bilateral conversations help the church reclaim and claim the doctrinal riches of its several heritages and to clarify its place within the boundaries of the orthodox faith. And, of course, the dialogues invite Methodist commitment to the breaking down of the longest-standing divisions in the Christian church, the reuniting with the church universal, and the establishment of the Methodist place therein.

The **multilateral or conciliar** fellowships function similarly, orienting Methodists to the widest possible Christian concord, possible only around the shared doctrinal witness of the ages. The World Council of Churches (WCC), National Council of Churches (NCC), and their state and local counterparts in the U.S. and abroad, also formally recognized by and financially undergirded by United Methodism, have claimed Methodist leadership from the start. In these ecumenical ventures,

Methodists have played instrumental roles and routinely served as their presidents. No one better epitomizes Methodist ecumenical agency than John R. Mott who led in the major cooperative/conciliar ventures from the Student Volunteer Movement (1888) to the World Council of Churches (1948). *Christian History* numbered Mott among "the ten most influential Christians of the twentieth century," the one Methodist to make that list.[19] Other Methodist saints who might be numbered in the conciliar, ecumenical fold are Frank Mason North, Francis J. McConnell, Ivan Lee Holt, G. Bromley Oxnam, Charles Parlin, William Cannon, J. Robert Nelson, John Deschner, Jeanne Audrey Powers, and William Grove. At this writing, Robert Edgar, previously President of Claremont School of Theology, has assumed the office of General Secretary of the NCC. He did so at a troubled time in the life of that institution and, while its troubles reflect unique developments, one might posit that the hopes for catholicity embodied in the conciliar fellowship appear more distant and claim less support. One wonders whether they might be re-energized and reclaim United Methodist interest were they to effect some rapprochement with their Evangelical/Pentecostal counterparts.

One conciliar effort, focused on U.S. churches, Churches Uniting in Christ (previously the Consultation on Church Union or COCU), has evolved from an effort at organic or institutional unity into a project of covenantal communion among its nine Protestant members (the Episcopal Church, the African Methodist Episcopal Church, the African Methodist Episcopal Zion Church, the Christian Church [Disciples of Christ], the Christian Methodist Episcopal Church, the International Council of Community Churches, the Presbyterian Church [USA], the United Church of Christ, and The United Methodist Church). This **national covenanting proposal** has been several times formally approved by General Conference. The 1996 General Conference, for instance, resolved to "adopt the covenanting proposal of the Consultation on Church Union and approve the text *Churches in Covenant Communion: The Church of Christ Uniting* as the basis for agreement to join with other participating churches in covenant communion" and "to enter into a relationship of Covenant Communion with the member churches of the Consultation on Church Union and other churches that similarly approve this agreement and *The COCU Consensus*, which is its theological basis, sealed by the proposed inaugural liturgies."[20] The *Consensus*, which United Methodists have affirmed, represents yet another witness to our catholic heritage.

One common religious enterprise, now not often numbered as such, would have been warmly embraced by U.S. United Methodists through much of the nineteenth and twentieth centuries. We speak of Methodist (that is MEC, MECS, MPC, UBC, and EA) involvement in the Protestant endeavor to **Christianize America**. Much of that agenda lives in **civil religious** residue.[21] Methodist efforts "to reform the Continent, and spread scriptural Holiness over these Lands"[22] initially did not command the respect of, nor renegotiate them into the religious establishment—formal and informal—of the early republic. But by the Civil War, Methodists did claim the respect and respectability of [23] and increasingly took a role in the unfolding campaign to build a Christian America. The war itself became part of the campaign, on both Yankee and Confederate sides. After the Civil War, laboring for a shared Protestant millennial ideal, Methodists channeled energies and resources into missions, into freedmen's aid, and into higher education. The latter, the United Methodist colleges and universities, perhaps best attest the effectiveness of Methodist efforts.[24] Equally powerfully, Methodists invested in the Protestantization of North American society through temperance and prohibition, an episode in U.S. history now remembered more ambiguously. Nevertheless, the catholic spirit of a Christian America remains deeply imprinted in United Methodist life. That spirit lives vibrantly in the church's "Social Creed" and "Social Principles,"[25] and in their application, 863 pages of which can be found in *The Book of Resolutions of The United Methodist Church, 2000*.

A different direction in catholicity, that of **global confessionalism**,[26] uniting the Methodist family, is represented by the World Methodist Council, another body in which United Methodism participates actively, indeed which it rather dominates. Headquartered at Lake Junaluska and long headed by Joe Hale, now by another United Methodist, George Freeman, the WMC connects United Methodism to the larger Methodist/Wesleyan family in North America and across the globe.[27] The WMC, established in 1951, institutionalized the gatherings at ten-year intervals (save in 1941) of "Ecumenical Methodist Conferences," the first of which convened at City Road Chapel, London, in 1881. These gatherings published their proceedings, but their greater deposit lay in the relations established among delegates and communions, and the encouragement developed there for other unitive efforts. The WMC continues these world plenaries, now on five year intervals. The WMC has sponsored important publishing ventures, including the *Journal and Letters of Francis Asbury* and the *Encyclopedia of World Methodism*. It also facilitates pulpit exchanges, endorses the Oxford Institute of Methodist Theological Studies, and publishes *World Parish*. My own school, Candler, benefits from one of its programs, World Evangelism, in our joint mounting of the World Methodist Evangelism Institute. The WMC achieves some measure of its authority and importance from its mirroring of other world confessional bodies and serving as their conversational partner in dialogues. The bilaterals, as noted, function under WMC sponsorship. The WMC might be a richer expression of United Methodism's catholicity, connectionalism, and global vision than the church concedes to it now.[28]

A related project in catholicity, **pan-Methodism,** seeks the restoration of relationships between United Methodism and the African Methodist churches (AME, AMEZ, CME). The term "pan-Methodism" has since the 1970s referred to conversations among these four churches, the formal establishment of a Commission on Pan-Methodist Cooperation in the late 1980s, and a Commission on Union organized in 1997 to guide formal exploration of merger. Here the separation to be overcome consists less in polity, practice, or precept than in scars left by the long saga of racism, discrimination, exploitation, and paternalism. As a healing gesture toward the separating wounds, the Commission, guided by GCCUIC and the UMC Council of Bishops, have made preparations for an Act of Repentance for Racism. At this writing, a study guide, "Steps Toward Wholeness: Learning and Repentance," has been published and made available on the GCCUIC Web site.[29]

Through a still more limited version of catholicity, **the global nature of the church**, United Methodism attempts to achieve parity, voice, and fuller inclusion in the life and governance of the denomination by the non-U.S. parts of the church. The emphasis has had signal leadership from the Council of Bishops, which has labored to achieve in its own life this spirit of catholicity, brought that emphasis to the church as a whole in its 1996 "Foundational Study: Global Nature of the Church," and transmitted that initiative to the 1996–2000 "Connectional Process" study. The church pursued much the same agenda in its efforts with Africa University, in the Russian evangelistic initiatives, and in starting work in South Africa.[30]

Perhaps in relation to the global nature of the church do the tensions between and among the several catholic directions emerge most clearly. By emphasizing its own global nature, United Methodism sometimes undercuts its interreligious, bilateral, and conciliar commitments with what other communions take as imperialistic actions; opts for a self-understanding that jeopardizes the World Methodist Council (global confessionalism); and raises questions about the seriousness of its unity ventures (pan-Methodism and CUIC [COCU]).

Yet another project in catholicity addresses the several forms of discord and disagreement that divide mainline Protestant denominations internally and ideologically. On a cluster of hot-button issues religious communities now find themselves in turmoil—school prayer, abortion, ordination of women, homosexuality, evolution, liberation theologies. For United Methodists, homosexuality and especially same-sex unions and ordination, have proved divisive. Persons with deep convictions on these issues take demonstrative actions, draft legislation in annual and general conferences, and organize themselves in caucuses. The communion polarizes. Charges and trials occasion greater stridency on both sides. Commentators and participants see the caucuses and struggle groups as balkanizing denominations, endangering their center and unity, and encouraging realignments that pull Christians into two broad coalitions, liberal and conservative.[31] Some project, others hope, that these denomination-transcending coalitions—liberal and conservative[32] or liberal and evangelical[33]—will divide, perhaps even destroy, denominations.[34] Working to overcome these tensions and impending division, GCCUIC has sponsored several **Diversity Dialogues**—deliberately constructed, several-day events, which brought together leaders from across the ideological spectrum for witness, listening, discernment, conversation, and community. Similar efforts have gone on in the Council of Bishops and in annual conferences. In them, Wesley's catholic spirit works preventively "to provide space for the Holy Spirit's work of discernment in The United Methodist Church and the lifting up of our essential unity in Christ in the midst of our disagreements."[35] The "discernment" employed in such efforts constitutes a style of leadership and decision-making, at least partially Quaker-inspired, that eschews votes and other divisive, winner-loser tactics in favor of efforts to recognize the spirit and wisdom of the whole.

Finally, one needs to speak of the caucus as a form of unity. The caucus structure, so effectively employed on the conservative side of the denomination (and the caucuses are several rather than just one), also functions well for those in various sectors of the denomination who seek common cause. The purposes vary. Koreans and Hispanics, persons interested in liturgy, charismatics, persons opposed to abortion, social activists, African Americans, and various others find unity and purpose in a caucus. The caucus gathers in regional and national celebrations, speaks its own "language," sings its commitments, publishes a newsletter, presses its concerns legislatively.[36] As noted above, we often view the caucus as divisive and in the sense that it divides into those within and without, it truly is. However, **the caucus** is itself a form of unity, a unity around purpose and cause. Its sense of urgency and priority, however, often makes it indifferent to our formal, institutionalized ecumenical endeavors. Christian unity has to take back seat to the caucus's own important agenda.

Contestation

In actual practice, then, the various kinds of unities, the various expressions of the catholic spirit, beckon the church in different directions. There is not one catholic or ecumenical future. Some United Methodists put their energies behind one pattern, others behind another.

If one participates, as have I recently, in a bilateral (with the Episcopal Church), one has less energy to invest in other forms of catholicity. Indeed, one experiences the other forms as something of a competition, even if, conceptually and eschatologically, one understands all forms of catholicity to cohere. Coherence ideally or in the endtime does not seem to dictate in the short run to whom to extend a hand, whom we believe to be joined with us in heart, and with whom we should partner theologically.

United Methodism has also had difficulty in getting the ecumenical or catholic message to its people (a problem not unique to us, I should add). The enthusiastic laborers for catholicity have come primarily from the higher echelons of denominational leadership—bishops, "professional" laity, a few seminary faculty, and the agency executives charged with unity and dialogue. Much of the ecumenical leadership trained itself in the institution-building that came out of the missionary endeavors of the nineteenth and early twentieth centuries. Some ecumenists worry as to whether the early generations of ecumenists will find progeny. Concern that younger leadership was not forthcoming has prompted GCCUIC to work zealously on seminaries to effect such a transmission of the ecumenical baton. Still, much of the church, including the new crop of seminarians, seems woefully ignorant of the church's existing ecumenical commitments. A query about CUIC (COCU), for instance, in a seminary class or with a group of otherwise informed and engaged laity, will draw absolutely blank looks. Ignorance and apathy compromise or frustrate Wesley's catholic and ecumenical mandate.

In addition, ecumenism proves to be itself divisive. United Methodism is indeed divided within, many United Methodists actively oppose ecumenical activity and the church's catholic commitments. The overt opposition to ecumenism tends to track or cohere with other concerns of the church's evangelical wing. Truth be told and as noted above, what outsiders discern in that opposition to institutionalized ecumenical endeavor is an alternative catholicity, one that unites evangelicals and conservatives in common social and political endeavor with counterparts in other denominations and in the political sector.[37] Some, then, along with kindred spirits in other denominations know well United Methodism's ecumenical activities, find them unacceptable, openly oppose involvement, especially in the NCC and WCC, and create their own unity through the Institute of Religion and Democracy and kindred organizations.

Others sharing a low priority for ecumenism are motivated by the new imperatives on disciple-making, evangelism, and mission. They would far more eagerly convert than cooperate. They see no problem in missionizing among peoples and in contexts where dialogue and ecumenical precept might counsel respect for existing religious commitments.

So, for a variety of reasons, United Methodism has gone on record and committed the denomination to an ecumenical and interreligious future, to a catholicity, that some United Methodist leaders and people fail to honor.

Still, the great middle of Methodism, though seldom as well informed about the church's actual catholic endeavors as they might be, support what they know. And they take pride in the leadership that Methodists provide ecumenical organizations on local, state, national, and world levels. Pride they can well take. At this writing, Methodists provide the chief presidential or executive officers to three of the most important ecumenical agencies—the WCC, NCC, and CUIC.

Understanding Catholicity Scripturally

Methodists have lived into and led the church's explorations of its catholicity. They have lived with the myriad texts that call the world into its wholeness in Christ. Of the many that might be appropriately examined, those that recall meals that Jesus ate with companions and those that point ahead to the eschatological banquet seem especially apt. Here I would note the narrative that connects so readily with the opening hymn and the vignette of Christian Newcomer, namely the end of Luke, the two on the way to Emmaus with the stranger. That text and Charles Wesley's refrain capture the connectional, disciplined, holy dimensions of Methodism's catholic hopes:

> HAPPY the souls to Jesus joined
> And saved by grace alone,
> Walking in all his ways they find
> Their heaven on earth begun.

A fellowship of the road, with strangers, eliciting a recalling and retelling of God's salvific acts, proclaiming that redemption to be offered to all, a breaking of bread in which promise becomes present, the recognition of

Christ in the gathering, and then the burning to be back on the road—that was Newcomer's story. And he told of a catholicity of Word and Table:

> Sunday 22d—An uncommonly large congregation had this day collected; I preached with great liberty from 1st Peter 5, v. 5 to 9. I was followed by a brother in the English language; a vast number came to the Lord's table, and we had a melting time. At night I preached again at John Buck's; here we again had a soul-reviving meeting; nearly every person present melted into tears; some cried for mercy, others shouted and praised God. 23d— This forenoon we held our Love-feast; we had truly a day of Pentecost: all the glory be to our God. I lodged with Rodebach. . . .

So Methodists, I suggest, find themselves on the road, offering and receiving hospitality, ecclesially, in the words of Luke:

> As they came near the village to which they were going, he walked ahead as if he were going on. But they urged him strongly, saying, "Stay with us, because it is almost evening and the day is now nearly over." So he went in to stay with them. When he was at the table with them, he took bread, blessed and broke it, and gave it to them. Then their eyes were opened, and they recognized him; and he vanished from their sight. . . . That same hour they got up and returned. (Luke 24:28-33)

Conclusion

The church: one, holy, catholic, and apostolic? as a past reality? to the eye today? or as the Christian hope? In Christ we know that the kingdom has come, the victory over sin and death won, a new reality initiated. Around our tables we experience and can bring others to experience that inbreaking eucharistic unity in and with Christ. We also look forward to an ultimate fulfillment, knowing that the church lives feebly and humanly in that new reality. So we sing with Charles Wesley, both proclaiming and awaiting the fullness of the church's catholicity and oneness:

> HAPPY the souls to Jesus joined, . . .
> The church triumphant in thy love,
> Their mighty joys we know; . . .
> Thee in thy glorious realm they praise,
> And bow before thy throne,
> We in the kingdom of thy grace:
> The kingdoms are but one.

As with the other marks—connectional, itinerant, disciplined—catholic represents a commitment and an ideal.

Postscript

These are the *principles* and *practices* of our sect; these are the *marks* of a true Methodist.[1] Connectional, disciplined, catholic, and itinerant—these four Methodist "marks" sustain key Wesley principles and practices, particularly his expectations and provisions for life together. The marks were faithfully implemented and institutionalized by early American Methodism.

The practices themselves have evolved in significant ways, becoming variously more complex, structured, diffused, differentiated over time. In the process, the relation between the evolving practices and the governing Wesleyan ideal, in different ways, has slipped, become strained, been disjoined. The Wesleyan rubrics, the terms or ideals, have tended to retain their simpler nuance (itinerant, catholic) or to denote only part of what the mark as practice has become (disciplined, connectional). The practices have changed dramatically as Methodism has grown from a small movement to a large, complex global institution. But the rubrics continue to have significant appeal with the people called Methodist.

At places United Methodism has been able to reach back, reclaim, and reinterpret the Wesleyan ideal, and stretch it to cover present institutional realities, reforming itself in the process. Something of that stretching can be seen in the bishops' efforts to refashion conferences into holy conferencing in the Wesleyan mode. That initiative reinvigorates the conference ideal and has the potential to enhance the quality of those basic United Methodist gatherings.

The prospect of such a recovery and refashioning seems to have guided the General Council on Ministries in three successive quadrennial studies of connectionalism and connectional governance. Each time the process brought forth a proposal for reforming the central structures of the church. Each proposal offered a vision of connectionalism and legislation to translate that vision into new structures of decision making. The three related but distinct efforts, though intriguing, failed to capture the imagination of General Conference. This third time (2004) apparently proved more than the delegates could take. The legislative committee crafted its own scheme, which involved abolishing the Council of Ministries and stream-lining decision making. General Conference passed the hastily developed efficiency plan, thus ending twelve and more years to reimagine connectionalism.

This saga leaves one wondering whether such restructuring, gargantuan in its potential scope and impact on denominational structure (1) can responsibly be undertaken in the short, frenzied atmosphere of

General Conference and (2) can really succeed without, as it were, addressing the other marks. Can United Methodism really reinspire itself connectionally, without reclaiming and reinvigorating discipline, catholicity, and itinerancy? Can and should it try to reinvigorate the marks separately? Or must it address them together? This query, asking us to think and rethink holistically, does not appear to have been posed and followed recently, if ever. It may be too much to ask that General Conference undertake such an integrative reclamation of our Wesleyan ideals. It may not be too much to hope that inspired lay and clergy leaders, agencies inclined to think beyond their own agenda, and the church's collegiate and seminary faculties could make various efforts at thinking holistically and ecclesiologically. If they do so we would urge attention to the guidance offered in the marks of Methodism.

The case for seeing these marks as an ecclesial whole, for seeing connectional, disciplined, catholic, and itinerant Methodist embodiments or enactments or institutionalizations of the traditional "notes" of the church, this volume opens rather than proves. We have suggested

- how American Methodism functioned with a connectionalism, that in its formation and reformations actualized and pointed to forms of oneness;
- how its discipline and disciplining sustained Wesleyan understandings of individual and corporate holiness;
- how its practices and publications oriented it to the catholic faith and to shared eucharistic meals; and
- how its missional, sent, itinerant ministry claimed and modeled an apostolic form, an affirmation early made about Methodist episcopacy.

As we have treated these four ecclesiology marks, we have also sought to show how those reference and entail other Wesleyan marks—connectionalism pointing to Methodism's forming and reforming impulse, discipline sustaining Methodism's holiness witness, catholicity vivifying Methodism's sacramental commitments, and itinerancy registering Methodism's own reading of apostolicity. Four more marks—oral/aural, evangelical/missionary, scriptural, and Arminian—shape and form all the marks as quadrilateral patterns of Methodist apprehending, knowing, and conveying.

Methodists never worked these practices or marks into an adequate systematic. In particular, we have not developed a coherent ecclesiology. However, proclaiming a Wesleyan version of the church's nature as one, holy, catholic, and apostolic, early Methodists held them together and did so with the rich nuances that each mark possessed. The case for their fullness and coherence as a practiced Methodist ecclesiology in an earlier chapter of our history, I hope I have made.

Revival?

To make the case for today that these practices "mark" us, that we have reclaimed and reinterpreted each mark in something of its fullness, that they function coherently and interactively, and that they together constitute an adequate embodied or practiced ecclesiology, we will need, I believe, to begin a sustained and collaborative effort to "read" our corporate life theologically and to seek to live into the fullness of our praxis. This volume has intended to show that such a reading is indeed possible.

If we attempt that, if we look closely at ourselves, either in the present, or the past, we can discover instructive patterns of theological faithfulness and Wesleyan doctrinal integrity. That careful reading, modeled here—with Scripture in hand, with a clear memory of what the Wesleys taught, and with our bearings set by the longer Christian witness—that careful reading will display, I believe, faithfulness, but also fragmentation.

As the two chapters with relatively recent vignettes should suggest (connectional and disciplined), careful institutional self-analysis can expose much of the full array of rich Wesleyan practiced ecclesiology. We also found that the Wesleyan mark, the term, no longer embraced that full array, that the practices had disengaged themselves from the Wesleyan term, that a mark's activities or practices had fragmented or been diffused, and that the Wesleyan principle's theological force had been squandered.

Were we to probe deeper with respect to any mark, we would find, I suspect, not only patterns of fragmentation, but also bureaucratization, politicization, inertia, indifference, decay, and even opposition. More grievously, we would find little in the way of cross-fertilization between and among the marks, even in our efforts at reform and reinvigoration. For instance, recent efforts to rethink ministry (itinerant) and governance (connectional) have been undertaken without cross-reference.[2] Efforts to revive us spiritually (disciplined) make little effort to engage the connection or recall our catholic witness. And, as we noted in the last chapter, the 2000 reaffirmation of the church's mission jostled and displaced our catholic self-affirmations in strange ways.

In our present life, though the Wesleyan practices live on, they do not cohere as marks nor collectively as a vision of the church. Or to put the problem more constructively, we make a quite adequate witness to these four ecclesial marks in Part II of the *Discipline,* "Doctrinal Standards and Our Theological Task." But we do not sustain that vision through the remainder of the *Discipline* nor live it out fully and coherently.

"What to Teach; How to Teach; and What to Do"

In this volume, we have endeavored to show that what we do and what we are doing, indeed, teaches—albeit not always clearly and cleanly. Methodism teaches in strange but authentic ways. Methodism teaches in its institutional life, in its structures, in its organizations, in its publications, in its initiatives, in its gatherings, in its practices. The oft-heard adage—practice what you preach, or your practice preaches—commonly applied to individuals, characterizes Methodism corporately. The "how" of our teaching, though we would not always claim it, is in our life together. And we have sought to make the case that if we inspect our corporate life carefully, we will find there our "What to Teach," namely both the Wesleyan missional, ecclesial witness and a full-orbed doctrine of the church. That we have work to do in bringing coherence to and drawing out that confession, I have just conceded.

These marks illustrate then a peculiar Methodist way of doing theology, of living in the great tradition, of remaining faithful to the Wesleys. They serve well to epitomize Methodism. These marks display nicely how Methodists embed fundamental Christian affirmations in practices, how Methodists practice what the Church, ecumenically and traditionally, has preached about itself, how Methodists do doctrine. *Religion in Life* we chose at one point as the title for what had been the *Methodist Quarterly Review,* now the *Quarterly Review.* Though apt, we might have proclaimed more assertively, "doctrine out of life."

To recognize our corporate life, even our institutional structures, as enacted theology should make us wary of unthinking or simply tactical change. Wesley's vaunted pragmatism did not embrace what worked just because it worked, but because in its workings he could recognize the Holy Spirit and a faithful expression of scriptural Christianity. My caution against sheer pragmatism should not discourage reform and renewal. Quite the opposite. To insist on the theological, even doctrinal, value of change orients us to seriousness about reform, about thinking and praying as we alter policy or structure, about renewal as a practiced mode of deep faithfulness. Faithful change re-inspires our connection, discipline, itinerancy, and catholicity.

The Quadrilateral

Much ink has been spilled recently over the quadrilateral. Some of the critique and some of the defense have viewed the quadrilateral as though it were doctrine, something in which to believe. So, also, commissioning and ordination interviews—at least in my experience—make the quadrilateral a faith matter. Committees seek from the person being grilled some assent to the quadrilateral or the primacy of scripture therein.

This exercise has endeavored to show that the quadrilateral offers a way of reading situation and event and structure and policy and practices and, of course, texts for theological and doctrinal affirmation. It is hermeneutic, not a doctrine. It posits that Methodist life itself, when true to itself, incarnates our belief. And it argues that one need not move directly from Scripture to doctrine to be a Scriptural Christian. That is the Calvinist pattern—doctrine out of the Word. The Calvinists move intellectually from Scripture. We move holistically from Scripture, with the whole self, indeed, the whole connection. And in so bringing Scripture into experience, we orient ourselves with tradition, both the great Christian tradition and our own Wesleyan witness. Of course, our intellect, our reason, also has play, guiding our decision making and testing our practices against the Word.

For Methodists, practices, policy, structure, event, and situation can disclose a faithful enactment of Scripture, a living of Scripture into life, an enfleshment or embodiment of Scripture.

When we look carefully we can find patterns of Scripture enfleshed or embodied. We can also find places where we have sinned and fallen short. When we so discern and confess, we might well seek faithfulness guided by "the marks of a true Methodist."

Appendix I

United Methodism and American Culture (UMAC)

Contents by Volume

UMAC Volume I
Connectionalism: Ecclesiology, Mission, and Identity (CEMI)

UMAC Volume III
Doctrines and Discipline (DD)

UMAC Volume IV
Questions for the Twenty-First Century
Church (QTCC)

PART ONE
"Where Will United Methodism Find Renewal
and Fulfill Its Mission?"

Appendix II

United Methodism and American Culture

Contributors of Volumes I-IV

Abbreviations

CEMI *Volume I:* Connectionalism: Ecclesiology, Mission, and Identity

PCM *Volume II:* The People(s) Called Methodist: Forms and Reforms of Their Life

DD *Volume III:* Doctrines and Discipline

QTCC *Volume IV:* Questions for the Twenty-First Century Church

Contributors

Becker, "Local Mission," *CEMI*, 267-85
Bell, "Homosexuality," *QTCC*, 271-79
Boomershine, "Electronic Culture," *QTCC*, 79-90
Bull, "Church Finance," *QTCC*, 280-86
Burton, "Media," *QTCC*, 91-104
Campbell, "Future," *QTCC*, 9-23
Campbell, "Introduction," *DD*, 1-15
Campbell, "To Elect Bishops," *QTCC*, 186-93
Campbell and Richey, "Annual Conference," *QTCC*, 301-12
Carroll, "Small Congregations," *QTCC*, 140-50
Carroll and Roof, "Congregations," *PCM*, 55-83
Cartwright, "Discipline," *DD*, 99-127
Chang, "Wages," *PCM*, 151-70
Everett and Frank, "Constitutional Order," *CEMI*, 41-73
Frank, "Common Discipline," *QTCC*, 219-31
González, "Hispanic United Methodists," *PCM*, 241-53
Gravely, "African-American in Memory," *PCM*, 175-90
Green and Guth, "Statistical Portrait," *PCM*, 27-52
Heitzenrater, "Connectionalism and Itinerancy," *CEMI*, 23-38
Herzog, "Missions," *DD*, 267-83
Jones, "Methodist Theology," *DD*, 77-95
Keller, "Moral Discourse," *DD*, 213-30
Kim, "Missions to Korea," *PCM*, 219-38
Kimbrough, "Music," *QTCC*, 24-37

Kreutziger, "Lay Leadership," *QTCC*, 119-31
Kreutziger, "Social Holiness," *CEMI*, 137-75
Langford, "Theology," *QTCC*, 45-50
Lawrence, "Clergy Leaders," *QTCC*, 132-39
Lawrence, "Introduction," *PCM*, 1-22
Lawrence, "Ordained Ministry," *QTCC*, 151-67
Lawrence and Froehlich, "Clergy Compensation," *QTCC*, 287-300
Longfield, "Methodist Identities," *CEMI*, 95-113
Love, "World Church," *QTCC*, 258-70
Maddox, "Untapped Inheritance," *DD*, 19-52
Marler and Hadaway, "'Self-Authoring' Religious Identity," *CEMI*, 289-316
Mathews, "Testimony, Voice," *PCM*, 279-304
McClain, "African American Methodists," *CEMI*, 77-91
McClain, "Preaching," *QTCC*, 168-74
Memming, "Ministry," *PCM*, 129-48
Monk, "Campus Ministry," *CEMI*, 179-202
Olson and McKinney, "Leaders," *PCM*, 109-26
O'Malley, "Distinctive Witness," *DD*, 53-76
Pope-Levison, "Evangelism," *QTCC*, 38-44
Quick, "The City," *QTCC*, 62-78
Richey, "Connectionalism," *QTCC*, 313-19
Richey, "Division," *QTCC*, 105-16
Richey, "Extension Ministries," *QTCC*, 175-85
Richey, "Introduction," *CEMI*, 1-20
Richey, "Twins," *QTCC*, 232-41
Robbins, "Connection," *DD*, 197-212
Rowe, "Caucuses," *QTCC*, 242-57
Rowe, "Redesigning Churches," *CEMI*, 117-34
Sano, "Contextual," *QTCC*, 51-61
Schneider, "Connectionalism," *DD*, 131-57
Shopshire, "Black Methodist Protestant," *PCM*, 193-216
Sledge, "Mergers," *CEMI*, 205-18
Smith, "Bishops," *QTCC*, 194-215
Strong, "Middle and Margins," *DD*, 233-41
Troxell and Farris, "One Eye," *PCM*, 257-73
Tucker, "Family and Midweek Worship," *DD*, 161-89
Watson, "Class Meetings" *DD*, 245-64
Wethington, "God's Mission," *CEMI*, 221-42
Wright, "Public Education," *DD*, 179-95
Zech, "Funding Crisis," *CEMI*, 245-64
Zech, "Giving," *PCM*, 87-105

Appendix III

Methodist Abbreviations

Denominations

AME   The African Methodist Episcopal Church (1816–)
AMEZ   The African Methodist Episcopal Church Zion (1820–)
CME   The (Colored) Christian Methodist Episcopal Church (1870–)
EA   The Evangelical Association/Church (1803–1946)
EUBC   The Evangelical United Brethren Church (1946–1968)
FMC   The Free Methodist Church (1860–)
MC   The Methodist Church, USA (1939–1968)
MEC   The Methodist Episcopal Church (1784–1939)
MECS   The Methodist Episcopal Church, South (1844–1939)
MPC   The Methodist Protestant Church (1830–1939)
UBC   The United Brethren Church (1800–1946)
UEC   The United Evangelical Church (1894–1922)
UMC   The United Methodist Church, USA (1968–)

Standard Publications

Asbury/Coke *Discipline* *The Doctrines and Discipline of the Methodist Episcopal Church in America, with Explanatory Notes by Thomas Coke and Francis Asbury* (Philadelphia, Pa.: Henry Tuckniss, 1798; reprint: Rutland, Vt.: Academy Books, 1979).

Bangs, *History* Nathan Bangs, *A History of the Methodist Episcopal Church*, 12th ed., 4 vols. (New York: Carlton & Porter, 1860).

Behney/Eller, *History* J. Bruce Behney & Paul H. Eller, *The History of the Evangelical United Brethren Church*, ed. Kenneth W. Krueger (Nashville: Abingdon, 1979).

Curts, *General Conferences* *The General Conferences of the Methodist Episcopal Church From 1792–1896*, edited by Lewis Curts (Cincinnati: Curts & Jennings, 1900).

Discipline/**church** The book of discipline (slightly varying names) for denomination named, with year specified; e.g., *Discipline*/UMC 1996.

Emory, *Discipline* Robert Emory, *History of the Discipline of the Methodist Episcopal Church*, rev. W. P. Strickland (New York: Carlton & Porter [1857]).

EWM *The Encylopedia of World Methodism,* 2 vols., edited by Nolan B. Harmon et al., sponsored by the World Methodist Council and the Commission on Archives and History, UMC (Nashville: United Methodist Publishing House, 1974).

HAM *The History of American Methodism,* ed. Emory S. Bucke, 3 vols. (New York & Nashville: Abingdon, 1964).

Hymnal/**church** Official hymnals for denomination named, with their year of first publication; e.g., *Hymnal* / AME 1984.

JLFA *The Journal and Letters of Francis Asbury,* ed. Elmer T. Clark, 3 vols. (London: Epworth, and Nashville: Abingdon, 1958).

JGC/MEC Refers to the *Journal of the General Conference of the Methodist Episcopal Church* for the year indicated. Includes citations from *Journals of the General Conference of the Methodist Episcopal Church, 1796–1856,* 3 vols. (New York: Carlton & Phillips, 1856). Vol. 1, 1796–1836; Vol. 2, 1840–1844; Vol. 3, 1848–1856.

JGC/MECS Refers to the *Journal of the General Conference of the Methodist Episcopal Church, South* for the year indicated. Includes citations from *Journals of the General Conference of the Methodist Episcopal Church, South, held 1846 and 1850* (Richmond: Published by John Early for the Methodist Episcopal Church, South).

JGC/MPC Refers to the *Journal of the . . . General Conference of the Methodist Protestant Church* for the year indicated.

Lee, *Short History* Jesse Lee, *A Short History of the Methodists* (Baltimore, 1810; Rutland, Vt.: Academy Books, 1974).

MEA *The Methodist Experience in America,* edited by Russell E. Richey, Kenneth E. Rowe, and Jean Miller Schmidt (Nashville: Abingdon Press, 2000).

Minutes/**church**/**year** Annual or General Minutes however titled and aggregated. Reference for the early years of the MEC is to *Minutes of the Annual Conferences of the Methodist Episcopal Church for the Years 1773–1828* (New York: T. Mason and G. Lane, 1840) unless alternative edition indicated. E.g. reference for 1784 in *Minutes of the Methodist Conferences, Annually Held in America; From 1773 to 1813, Inclusive* (New York:

Published by Daniel Hitt & Thomas Ware for the Methodist Connexion in The United States, 1813) as *Minutes*/MEC/1784 (1813).

Perspectives *Perspectives on American Methodism*, edited by Russell E. Richey, Kenneth E. Rowe, and Jean Miller Schmidt (Nashville: Kingswood Books, 1993).

Richey, *Conference* Russell E. Richey, *The Methodist Conference in America* (Nashville: Kingswood Books, 1996).

Sweet, *Methodists* William Warren Sweet, ed., *Religion on the American Frontier, 1783–1840: The Methodists, A Collection of Source Materials* (New York: Cooper Square [1964]; reprint of 1946 edition).

Tigert, History John J. Tigert, *A Constitutional History of American Episcopal Methodism*, 3rd ed., revised and enlarged (Nashville: Publishing House of the Methodist Episcopal Church, South, 1908).

Wesley Materials

Chr. Library *A Christian Library: Consisting of Extracts from, and Abridgements of, the Choicest Pieces of Practical Divinity which have been Published in the English Tongue,* 50 vols. (Bristol: F. Farley, 1749–55; reprinted in 30 vols., London: T. Cordeux, 1819–27).

Hymns, Works 7 *A Collection of Hymns for the Use of the People Called Methodists,* edited by Franz Hildebrandt and Oliver Beckerlegge (Nashville: Abingdon, 1983); volume 7 of *Works.*

Letters (Telford) *The Letters of the Rev. John Wesley, A.M.,* edited by John Telford, 8 vols. (London: Epworth, 1931) [NB: Use only for letters dated after 1755].

Sunday Service *The Sunday Service of the Methodists in North America* (London: Strahan, 1784; reprint ed., Nashville: United Methodist Publishing House, 1992).

Works *The Works of John Wesley*; begun as "The Oxford Edition of The Works of John Wesley" (Oxford: Clarendon Press, 1975–1983); continued as "The Bicentennial Edition of The Works of John Wesley" (Nashville: Abingdon, 1984—); 16 of 35 vols. published to date.

Works (Jackson) *The Works of John Wesley,* ed. Thomas Jackson, 14 vols. (London, 1872; Grand Rapids: Zondervan, 1958).

Notes

Preface

1. The phrase derives from Albert C. Outler, who wrote *Theology in the Wesleyan Spirit* (Nashville: Tidings, 1975) and earlier *Evangelism in the Wesleyan Spirit* (Nashville: Tidings, 1971). For references on religious practices, please consult notes in the introduction.

Introduction

1. See, for instance, Robert E. Cushman, *John Wesley's Experimental Divinity: Studies in Methodist Doctrinal Standards* (Nashville: Kingswood Books/Abingdon Press, 1989); Thomas A. Langford, *Practical Divinity: Theology in the Wesleyan Tradition* (Nashville: Abingdon Press, 1983); Scott J. Jones, *United Methodist Doctrine: The Extreme Center* (Nashville: Abingdon Press, 2002), 61, 71-77, 241-97; Kenneth J. Collins, *A Real Christian: The Life of John Wesley* (Nashville: Abingdon Press, 1999).

2. See "Dialogue participants share views on what unites, divides the church," United Methodist News Service, Nov. 24, 1997, http://www.umc.org/umns/news97/nov/tissues.htm. We return below to discuss this item and the released text. On the enduring Wesleyan emphases, see Maddox, "Untapped Inheritance," *DD*, 19-52. For abbreviations employed to reference essays in the United Methodism and American Culture (UMAC) series, see the appendices.

3. See, for instance, Craig Dykstra, *Growing in the Life of Faith: Education and Christian Practices* (Louisville, Ky.: Geneva Press, 1999); Margaret Miles, *Practicing Christianity: Critical Perspectives for an Embodied Spirituality* (New York: Crossroad, 1988); Dorothy Bass, ed., *Practicing Our Faith: A Way of Life for a Searching People* (San Francisco: Jossey-Bass, 1997); Miroslav Volf and Dorothy C. Bass, eds., *Practicing Theology: Beliefs and Practices in Christian Life* (Grand Rapids, Mich.: William B. Eerdmans, 2002); Jones, "Methodist Theology," *DD*, 77-95. For further items, see the Web site for the Valparaiso Project: www.practicingourfaith.org.

4. *The Bicentennial Edition of the Works of John Wesley* (Nashville: Abingdon Press, 1984-), vol. 9 *The Methodist Societies: History, Nature, and Design*, ed. Rupert E. Davies, 30-46. The entire volume bears on the approach we are outlining. This edition will be referenced simply as *Works*.

5. The UMNS release continued:

Points of disunity fell generally into categories related to the authority of scripture, essential doctrines, matters of conscience and an understanding of mission. Specific items listed, again in no order of importance, included:

- doctrine, dogma and essentials of the faith;
- lack of agreement about how doctrine interacts with theology;
- different views about source of religious authority, specifically scripture;
- how sin is understood and dealt with;
- differences in theology;

- scripture and biblical authority;
- reasons given for loss in membership;
- authority of Social Principles;
- sexuality, including homosexuality;
- stereotyping, misrepresentations, name-calling;
- community vs. individual conscience as illustrated by responses to actions taken by the General Conference;
- alienation of people who feel disenfranchised, including evangelicals and homosexual people;
- "non-negotiable" essentials of the faith including the divinity of Jesus Christ;
- mission and how it is done around the world;
- role of bishops and understanding of the episcopal office;
- language, particularly the traditional reference to the trinity (Father, Son, and Holy Ghost);
- relationship of church to culture;
- role and authority of General Conference.

Several items fell in both categories of issues that unite and threaten unity. They included the relationship between personal piety and social holiness and what often is referred to as the Wesleyan quadrilateral. The latter is found in the "Our Theological Task" portion of the church's *Book of Discipline*. It encourages United Methodists to do theology, keeping in tension Scripture, tradition, experience, and reason. The most significant issue surfaced here related to the primacy of scripture within the quadrilateral formulation.

Before the close of their first meeting, participants began to discuss what would be necessary for the unity of the church to be sustained and disunity avoided. Suggestions from individual participants, included:

- accountability of general agencies to General Conference;
- accountability of bishops to support General Conference actions;
- consensus on central doctrines of the church;
- celebration of differences without compromising basic theological foundations;
- openness to the Holy Spirit as old truths are formulated in new metaphors and language;
- greater trust and mutual respect;
- toned down rhetoric and stereotyping;
- willingness to listen;
- membership of General Conference related to population of church;
- acceptance of the authority of scripture;
- cessation of press conferences and reports that seem to take isolated occurrences and make them look like widespread happenings;
- development of consensus on mission and work of the church as a whole;
- genuine compassion for people who may be hurt by the positions taken by the church, specifically gay and lesbian Christians;
- meaning of the lordship of Jesus Christ;
- trusted, credible forum to discuss differing theological issues;

- willingness to coexist;
- discipleship that reflects a desire for shared standards of beliefs, not just description of some thoughts and feelings;
- bishop and district superintendents cease punitive actions against congregations and pastors who can't, because of conscience support giving to apportionments which support some church agencies;
- renewal of the office of bishop as crucial agent for unity of the whole church;
- restraint in the use of inflammatory rhetoric and institutional power to silence and stigmatize individuals who disagree.

Source: http://www.umc.org/umns/news97/nov/tissues.htm
"Dialogue participants share views on what unites, divides the church" United Methodist News Service, Nov. 24, 1997. Used with permission.

6. *Formal Fraternity. Proceedings of the General Conference of the Methodist Episcopal Church and of the Methodist Episcopal Church, South. In 1872, 1874, and 1876. And of the Joint Commission of the Two Churches on Fraternal Relations. At Cape May, New Jersey. August 16-23, 1876* (New York: Nelson & Phillips; Nashville: A. H. Redford, 1876), 81-82. The two churches preceded the cited statement with the affirmation:

> We cannot restrain the expression of our united congratulations to both of the great Churches whose Commissions we have executed, in uniting between them the broken cords of affectionate and brotherly fraternization. Henceforth they may hail each other as from the auxiliary ranks of one great army. The only differences they will foster will be those friendly rivalries that spring from earnest endeavors to further to the utmost the triumphs of the gospel of peace. Whatever progress is made by the one Church or by the other will occasion general joy. They will rejoice in each other's success as a common good; and, amid the thousand glorious memories of Methodism, they will go forward devoted to their one work of spreading Scriptural holiness over these lands.

The two churches went on then to affirm:

> Far away in dark portions of the earth, to which their missionaries have penetrated, a divine light is breaking on the long night of paganism. For the elevation of humanity, it is more than the wand of an enchanter. There, as well as here, Methodist doctrines and usages wear their own peculiar and heaven-blessed distinctiveness, and seem to presage the dawn of that era of gladness when the claims of universal brotherhood will commingle with the full glory of the millennium. Episcopal Methodism was never more strong and influential, and never appeared to feel more the quickening impulse of its glorious destiny, than it does at the present day.

7. See *A Record of All Agreements Concerning Fraternity and Federation Between the Methodist Episcopal Church and the Methodist Episcopal Church, South* (Nashville: Publishing House of the Methodist Episcopal Church, South, 1914); Thomas B. Neely, *American Methodism: Its Divisions and Unification* (New York: Fleming H. Revell

Company, 1915); *A Working Conference on the Union of American Methodism, Northwestern University* (New York: Methodist Book Concern, 1916); Paul N. Garber, *The Methodists Are One People* (Nashville: Cokesbury Press, 1939); John M. Moore, *The Long Road to Methodist Union* (Nashville: The Methodist Publishing House, 1948); James H. Straughn, *Inside Methodist Union* (Nashville: The Methodist Publishing House, 1958); Frederick E. Maser, "The Story of Unification, 1874–1939," HAM, III, 407-78; Walter G. Muelder, *Methodism and Society in the Twentieth Century*, Methodism and Society, II (New York and Nashville: Abingdon Press, 1961), 251-71; Nolan B. Harmon, *The Organization of the Methodist Church*, 2nd rev. ed. (Nashville: Methodist Publishing House, 1962), 167-82; Robert Watson Sledge, *Hands on the Ark. The Struggle for Change in the Methodist Episcopal Church, South, 1914–1939* (Lake Junaluska, N.C.: Commission on Archives and History, UMC, 1975), 90-123; Grant S. Shockley, ed., *Heritage and Hope: The African-American Presence in United Methodism* (Nashville: Abingdon Press, 1991); William B. McClain, *Black People in the Methodist Church* (Cambridge: Schenkman Publishing Co., 1984); James S. Thomas, *Methodism's Racial Dilemma: The Story of the Central Jurisdiction* (Nashville: Abingdon Press, 1992).

8. See the eight *Proceedings of the Oecumenical Methodist Conference, 1876–1951* and *Proceedings of the World Methodist Conference, 1956–*.

9. Cincinnati: The Methodist Publishing House, 1947.

10. Nashville: Methodist Evangelistic Materials, 1960.

11. See James E. Kirby, *Brother Will: A Biography of William C. Martin* (Nashville: Abingdon Press, 2000), 329. Mary Elizabeth Moore, "The Style and Substance of United Methodist Theology in Transition," in Thomas A. Langford, ed., *Doctrine and Theology in The United Methodist Church* (Nashville: Kingswood Books/Abingdon Press, 1991), 208-22. Her phrasing differs slightly from our representation of it.

12. (Nashville: Abingdon Press, 2004). The practices constitute chapter titles.

13. See, for instance, Abel Stevens, *The Centenary of American Methodism: A Sketch of its History, Theology, Practical System and Success*, prepared by Order of the Centenary Committee of the General Conference of the Methodist Episcopal Church (New York: Carlton & Porter, 1865); or James Porter, *The Revised Compendium of Methodism* (New York: Hunt & Eaton; Cincinnati: Cranston & Stowe, 1875).

14. This phrase by which we point to the considerable attention recently paid American Methodism we selected for the title and the findings of our Lilly Endowment sponsored project, United Methodism and American Culture [UMAC], undertaken while the three of us were faculty members and administrators at Duke Divinity School. This project involved a significant assemblage of church leaders and academics, several conferences and a considerable output of presentations and essays. The research done under Lilly auspices appeared in the first four volumes of this series and is represented in the Tables of Contents in Appendix I. Appendix II represents those essays, arrayed alphabetically by author and with the abbreviated title we use in notes.

15. See Maddox, "Untapped Inheritance," *DD*, 19-52; Langford, "Theology," *QTCC*, 45-50; Sano, "Contextual," *QTCC*, 51-61.

16. As the three of us worked through the several volumes of the UMAC project, in the editing processes and as we returned to the essays to think about synthetic themes, we both recognized the full array of marks and discerned that four of these essentials proved most apt for capturing the findings of our scholars and their essays.

17. These four, we think, also most fully and consistently captured our UMAC research. The UMAC studies and the published essays as a whole pointed, we thought, to these four. Several essays, in particular, prove helpful in understanding this Wesleyan gestalt. See especially Robbins, "Connection," *DD*, 197-212; Heitzenrater, "Connectionalism and Itinerancy," *CEMI*, 23-38; Richey, "Connectionalism," *QTCC*, 313-19; Richey, "Introduction," *CEMI*, 1-20.

18. For elaboration of Methodism's Arminian theology, see the works cited in note 1 or the treatment in the *Discipline*, Part II covering our doctrine and doctrinal heritage.

19. See Mathews, "Testimony, Voice," *PCM*, 279-304; Tucker, "Family and Midweek Worship," *DD*, 161-89; and Kimbrough, "Music," *QTCC*, 24-37.

20. *Works*, 7:698-99, # 507, [The Love-feast] Part III.

21. *The Works of the Rev. John Wesley, A.M.*, ed. Thomas Jackson, 14 vols. (London: Wesleyan Conference Office, 1872), VIII, 275.

22. See the work of friends, Ted A. Campbell, *Methodist Doctrine: The Essentials* (Nashville: Abingdon Press, 1999); Scott J. Jones, *United Methodist Doctrine: The Extreme Center*; and Walter Klaiber and Manfred Marquardt, *Living Grace: An Outline of United Methodist Theology*, translated and adapted by J. Steven O'Malley and Ulrike R. M. Guthrie (Nashville: Abingdon Press, 2001).

23. But see Thomas Edward Frank, *Polity, Practice, and the Mission of The United Methodist Church* (Nashville: Abingdon Press, 1997) and Henry H. Knight III, *Eight Life-Enriching Practices of United Methodists* (Nashville: Abingdon Press, 2001).

24. *Works*, 7:3, 55-61, 74, 77-78. See Karen B. Westerfield Tucker, *American Methodist Worship* (New York: Oxford University Press, 2001), 156-75.

25. Here we might note a companion effort to read practices and particularly religious organization as theologically suggestive and important. This is the Hartford Seminary study "Organizing Religious Work," one result of which will appear as *Denominational Identities in Unsettled Times: Theology, Structure and Change*, David A. Roozen and James Nieman, eds. (Grand Rapids: William B. Eerdmans, forthcoming). Richey, James Wood, and Pamela Couture undertake exploration of United Methodist organization and organizational change.

26. O'Malley, "Distinctive Witness," *DD*, 53-76.

27. On the development of the 1972 and 1988 Disciplinary Statements, see Thomas A. Langford, ed., *Doctrine and Theology in The United Methodist Church* (Nashville: Kingswood Books/Abingdon Press, 1991).

28. See Ted A. Campbell, "The 'Wesleyan Quadrilateral': The Story of a Modern Methodist Myth," and Albert C. Outler, "The Wesleyan Quadrilateral—In John Wesley," in Langford, ed., *Doctrine and Theology in The United Methodist Church*, 154-61 and 75-88; W. Stephen Gunter et al., *Wesley and the Quadrilateral: Renewing the Conversation* (Nashville: Abingdon Press, 1997); Scott J. Jones, *John Wesley's Conception and Use of Scripture* (Nashville: Kingswood Books/Abingdon Press, 1995); Scott J. Jones, *United Methodist Doctrine: The Extreme Center*; and Walter Klaiber and Manfred Marquardt, *Living Grace: An Outline of United Methodist Theology*, translated and adapted by J. Steven O'Malley and Ulrike R. M. Guthrie (Nashville: Abingdon Press, 2001), 17-92.

29. See Klaiber and Marquardt, *Living Grace: An Outline of United Methodist Theology*, 27-35.

30. Compare Theodore Runyon, *The New Creation: John Wesley's Theology Today* (Nashville: Abingdon Press, 1998); Ted A. Campbell, *Methodist Doctrine: The Essentials* (Nashville: Abingdon Press, 1999); Jones, *United Methodist Doctrine: The Extreme Center*; and Walter Klaiber and Manfred Marquardt, *Living Grace: An Outline of United Methodist Theology.*

31. *Works*, 9:41.

1. Connectional

1. *Hymns,* Works, 7:712-13, #520.

2. Asbury/Coke, *Discipline* (1798), 52.

3. George G. Cookman, *Speeches Delivered on Various Occasions* (New York: George Lane for the MEC, 1840), 145-47. *From Methodist Experience in America: A Sourcebook.*

4. *A Compendious History of American Methodism* (New York: Eaton & Mains, n.d. but 1868/67), 19. Stevens's *History of the Methodist Episcopal Church* 4 vols. (New York: Carlton & Porter, 1864–67) began with the same scene but lacked the chapter title.

5. Leo Marx makes no space for Methodism in his *Machine in the Garden: Technology and the Pastoral Ideal in America* (London, Oxford, and New York: Oxford University Press, 1964). His image fit Methodism perfectly.

6. See William McGuire King, "Denominational Modernization and Religious Identity: The Case of the Methodist Episcopal Church," in *Perspectives*, 343-55.

7. Worth M. Tippy and Paul B. Kern, *A Methodist Church and Its Work* (New York and Cincinnati: The Methodist Book Concern; Nashville: Lamar & Barton, 1919), 90.

8. See Stephen Perry, "The Revival of Stewardship and the Creation of the World Service Commission in the Methodist Episcopal Church, 1912–1924," *Perspectives*, 400-14.

9. United Methodist News Service {210}. Used with UMNS permission. Green is news writer of UMNS's Nashville, Tenn., office. Source: http://umc.org/umns/99/apr/210.htm. Paragraphing altered to suit vignette format.

10. Minton Thrift, *Memoir of the Rev. Jesse Lee. With Extracts from His Journals* (New York: N. Bangs and T. Mason for the Methodist Episcopal Church, 1823), 42.

11. Watson, "Class Meetings," *DD.*

12. The entirety of our first volume, *CEMI*, bears on this discussion. See particularly the introduction. See also Robbins, "Connection," *DD*, 197-212, Campbell and Richey, "Annual Conference," *QTCC*, 301-12, and Richey, "Connectionalism," *QTCC*, 313-19.

13. On the festival and eucharistic character of early Methodist gatherings see my *The Methodist Conference in America: A History* (Nashville: Kingswood Books/Abingdon Press, 1996) and *Early American Methodism* (Bloomington: Indiana University Press, 1991) and Lester Ruth, *A Little Heaven Below: Worship at Early American Methodist Quarterly Meetings* (Nashville: Kingswood Books/Abingdon Press, 2000).

14. For a different ordering of these points about connectionalism, see "Introduction," *CEMI*. On the first point, see Heitzenrater, "Connectionalism and Itinerancy," *CEMI*, 23-38.

15. See "Introduction," *CEMI*, 3-4; Campbell and Richey, "Annual Conference," *QTCC*, 303-5.

16. Heitzenrater, "Connectionalism and Itinerary," *CEMI*.

17. Robert D. Putnam, *Bowling Alone: The Collapse and Revival of American Community* (New York: Simon & Schuster, 2000), and Robert D. Butler and Lewis M. Feldstein, with Don Cohen, *Better Together: Restoring the American Community* (New York: Simon & Schuster, 2003).

18. Campbell and Richey, "Annual Conference," *QTCC*, 301-12.

19. See Quick, "The City," *QTCC*, 62-78; Wright, "Public Education," *DD*, 179-95; Richey, "Extension Ministries," *QTCC*, 175-85; Kreutziger, "Social Holiness," *CEMI*, 137-75 and "Lay Leadership," *QTCC*, 119-31; Monk, "Campus Ministry," *CEMI*, 179-202; Watson, "Class Meetings," *DD*, 245-64; Herzog, "Missions," *DD*, 267-83; Wethington,"God's Mission," *CEMI*, 221-42; Boomershine, "Electronic Culture," *QTCC*, 79-90.

20. Kreutziger, "Lay Leadership," *QTCC*, 119-31 and "Social Holiness," *CEMI*, 137-75; Troxell and Farris, "One Eye," *PCM*, 257-73.

21. Richey, "Introduction," 8-20, and Everett and Frank, "Constitutional Order," 41-73, *CEMI*. Richey, "Twins" and "Connectionalism" in *QTCC*.

22. Richey, "Twins," *QTCC*.

23. Becker, "Local Mission," *CEMI*, 265-85.

24. Boomershine, "Electronic Culture," *QTCC*, 79-90.

25. Burton, "Media," *QTCC*, 91-104.

26. Love, "World Church," *QTCC*, 258-70. See also Wethington, "God's Mission," *CEMI* and Herzog, "Missions," *DD*.

27. For a recent reiteration of this point, see Winthrop S. Hudson and John Corrigan, *Religion in America*, 6th ed. (Upper Saddle River, N.J.: Prentice Hall, 1999), 136-39.

28. Richey, "Extension Ministries," *QTCC*, esp. 185.

29. Rowe, "Caucuses," *QTCC*, 242-57; González, "Hispanic United Methodists," *PCM*, 241-53.

30. Rowe, "Caucuses," *QTCC*, 251-66. See also Richey, "Division," *QTCC*, 105-16.

31. Zech, "Funding Crisis," *CEMI*, 245-64 and "Giving," *PCM*, 87-105.

32. Bull, "Church Finance," *QTCC*, 280-86.

33. Wethington, "God's Mission," *CEMI*, 221-42; Herzog, "Missions," *DD*.

34. See especially Watson, "Class Meetings," *DD*.

35. James K. Mathews and William B. Oden, eds., *Vision and Supervision: A Sourcebook of Significant Documents of the Council of Bishops of The United Methodist Church* (Nashville: Abingdon Press, 2003); Roy Hunter Short, *Chosen to Be Consecrated: The Bishops of The Methodist Church, 1784–1968* (Lake Junaluska, N.C.: Commission on Archives and History for the Council of Bishops, 1976), esp. 23-49; James E. Kirby, Russell E. Richey, and Kenneth E. Rowe, *The Methodists* (Westport, Conn.: Greenwood Press, 1996), 48-55; James E. Kirby, *The Episcopacy in American Methodism* (Nashville: Kingswood Books/Abingdon Press, 2000); Russell E. Richey and Thomas Edward Frank, *Episcopacy in the Methodist Tradition: Perspectives and Proposals* (Nashville: Abingdon Press, 2004).

36. Smith, "Bishops," *QTCC*, 194-215. These generalizations also derive from an off-the-record session of retired or retiring bishops with UMAC principals in the final phase of the grant study.

37. Frank, "Common Discipline," *QTCC*, 227-29.

38. Asbury/Coke, *Discipline* (1798), 41-42.

39. Frank, "Common Discipline," QTCC, 232-34.

40. Heitzenrater, "Connectionalism and Itinerancy," *CEMI*, 35.

41. Pope-Levison, "Evangelism," QTCC, 38-44.

42. An essay of mine on this topic, "District Superintendency: A Reconsideration," is forthcoming.

43. Tigert, *History*, juxtaposes the "Large Minutes" and first *Discipline* (534-602, 535) Wesley's answer had been "to reform the Nation, particularly the Church; and to spread scriptural holiness over the land."

44. Campbell, "Future," *QTCC*, 9-23; Lawrence, "Introduction," *PCM*, 1-22.

45. Richey, "Introduction," *CEMI*, 1-20; Everett and Frank, "Constitutional Order," *CEMI*, 41-73; Richey, "Connectionalism," *QTCC*, 313-19; "Twins," *QTCC*, 232-41; Kim, "Missions to Korea," *PCM*, 219-38.

46. Kreutziger, "Social Holiness," *CEMI*, 137-75 and "Lay Leadership," 119-31.

47. Quick, "The City," *QTCC*, 62-78. Quick laments the absence of such a national urban strategy within United Methodism today.

48. See Richard P. Heitzenrater, *Wesley and the People Called Methodists* (Nashville: Abingdon Press, 1995), especially 97-198.

49. Everett and Frank, "Constitutional Order," *CEMI*, 41-73.

50. See Richey, "Introduction," *CEMI*, 3-4 and *Early American Methodism*, 65-81.

51. Campbell, "To Elect Bishops," *QTCC*, 186-93; Richey, "Connectionalism," *QTCC*, 313-19.

52. Love, "World Church," *QTCC*, 258-70.

53. Campbell, "Future," *QTCC*, 9-23.

54. Frank, "Common Discipline," *QTCC*, 219-31; Becker, "Local Mission," *CEMI*, 267-85.

55. *Minutes of the Methodist Conferences, annually held in America from 1773 to 1784, inclusive* (Philadelphia: Printed by Henry Tuckniss; sold by John Dickins, 1795), 5-7.

56. McClain, "African American Methodists," *CEMI*, 77-91; Gravely, "African-American in Memory," *PCM*, 175-90; Cartwright, "Discipline," *DD*, 99-127; Mathews, "Testimony, Voice," *PCM*, 279-304; Shopshire, "Black Methodist Protestant," *PCM*, 193-216; Schneider, "Connectionalism," *DD*, 131-57; Longfield, "Methodist Identities," *CEMI*, 95-113; Strong, "Middle and Margins," *DD*, 233-41; Richey, "Division," *QTCC*, 105-16.

57. See the essays in *DD* by Maddox, "Untapped Inheritance," 19-52 and Jones, "Methodist Theology," 79-95; and in *QTCC*, Langford, "Theology," 45-50 and Sano, "Contextual," 51-61.

58. Quick, "The City," *QTCC*, 62-78; Wright, "Public Education," *DD*, 179-95; Richey, "Extension Ministries," *QTCC*, 175-85; Kreutziger, "Social Holiness," *CEMI*, 137-75 and "Lay Leadership," *QTCC*, 119-31; Monk, "Campus Ministry," *CEMI*, 179-202; Watson, "Class Meetings," *DD*, 245-64; Herzog, "Missions," *DD*, 267-83; Wethington, "God's Mission," *CEMI*, 221-42; Boomershine, "Electronic Culture," *QTCC*, 79-90.

59. Smith, "Bishops," *QTCC*, 194-215.

60. *Discipline*/UMC 1992, Sect. 112, pp. 111-14; *Discipline*/UMC 1988, Sect. 112, pp. 116-18. In 1996, General Conference reduced that section to two very short paragraphs, replacing it, in effect, by an extended discussion of "Servant Ministry and

Servant Leadership." *Discipline*/UMC 1996, Sects., 109-16, pp. 109-12. For an excellent discussion of this section and its import, see Robbins, "Connection," *DD*, 197-212. The following discussion builds on his insights.

61. See Frank, "Common Discipline," *QTCC*, 219-31, on the 1996 *Discipline* and the changes it wrought, including its functionalism; the permission to disengage forms at the several levels; the relation of connectionalism and ecclesiology; connectionalism, discipline, and Discipline; the chaos resulting from removing a common organizational grammar; and the ambiguity about what constitutes the connection at the local level.

2. Itinerant

1. *Hymns for the Use of the Methodist Episcopal Church*, rev. ed. (New York: Carlton & Porter, 1849), 133, #214. Marked S.M. Acts xxviii. 31. A Charles Wesley hymn not included in *Works* 7.

2. Methodists have employed both itinerancy and itineracy. The terms are interchangeable. Here the former is used.

3. See *The Journal and Letters of Francis Asbury*, ed. Elmer T. Clark, 3 vols. (London and Nashville: Epworth Press & Abingdon Press, 1958). For a recent review of Asbury's missionary activities, see Darius L. Salter, *America's Bishop: The Life of Francis Asbury* (Nappanee, Ind.: Francis Asbury Press of Evangel Publishing House, 2003).

4. *A Journal of the Travels of William Colbert, Methodist Preacher: thro' parts of Maryland, Pennsylvania, New York, Delaware and Virginia in 1790 to 1838*, 10 vols. typescript. Used at Drew University. II: 164-71. On Colbert's career and the dimensions of his traveling commented on here, see Warren S. Napier, *Formed for Friendship: Revisioning Early American Circuit Riders Through the Journal of William Colbert, 1790–1833*, Ph.D. Dissertation, Iliff School of Theology and The University of Denver, 1996. The omissions (. . . .) allow us to exhibit the sustained pattern of his travel without all the detail that follows. Information within brackets [ ] has been added.

5. The traveling ministry was, at this juncture, entirely male, and pronouns are introduced accordingly.

6. See Heitzenrater, "Connectionalism and Itinerancy," *CEMI*; Lawrence, "Ordained Ministry," *QTCC*; and Campbell, *The Yoke of Obedience: The Meaning of Ordination in Methodism* (Nashville: Abingdon Press, 1988). For questions as to whether ministry retains this missional aspect, see Lawrence and Froehlich, "Clergy Compensation," *QTCC*.

7. Frank, "Common Discipline," *QTCC*, 219-31.

8. Russell E. Richey, Kenneth E. Rowe, and Jean Miller Schmidt, *The Methodist Experience in America: A Sourcebook*, II (Nashville: Abingdon Press, 2000), 1784a, 123-31 (hereafter this volume is abbreviated MEA); excerpted from Thomas Coke and Francis Asbury's annotated *Discipline*. Asbury/Coke, *Discipline* (1798), 42.

9. See Heitzenrater, "Connectionalism and Itinerancy," *CEMI*.

10. In shortening the selection from Colbert, I have omitted the scripture texts that Colbert almost always noted for persons and noted for others as well as for himself. Those notations show that contrary to a common misapprehension, the itinerants did not preach the same sermon through a circuit or at least they did not start their

sermons from the same text. Having comrades on the road with them doubtless encouraged the itinerants to some variety of text and message.

11. Frank, "Common Discipline," *QTCC*, 232-33. Lawrence calls for the church today to think about itinerancy less as a matter of mobility and more in theological, inclusive, connectional, and pragmatic terms. Lawrence, "Ordained Ministry," *QTCC*.

12. Asbury/Coke, *Discipline* (1798), 35-36.

13. For the text of the first *Discipline* in parallel columns with the "Large Minutes" see Tigert, *History*. Citation from 549. By 1798 when the bishops annotated the *Discipline* the question read:

> Quest. If the bishop cease from travelling at large among the people, shall he still exercise his office among us in any degree?
>
> Answ. If he cease from travelling without the consent of the general conference, he shall not hereafter exercise any ministerial function whatsoever in our church. Asbury/Coke, *Discipline*, (1798), 39.

14. Asbury/Coke, *Discipline* (1798), 44-45.

15. On Methodist understandings and practices of episcopacy, see James E. Kirby, *The Episcopacy in American Methodism* (Nashville: Kingswood Books/Abingdon Press, 2000); Gerald F. Moede, *The Office of Bishop in Methodism: Its History and Development* (Zurich, New York, and Nashville: Abingdon Press, 1964); James K. Mathews, *Set Apart to Serve: The Meaning and Role of Episcopacy in the Wesleyan Tradition* (Nashville: Abingdon Press, 1985); Gerald F. Moede, "Bishops in the Methodist Tradition: Historical Perspectives," *Episcopacy: Lutheran-United Methodist Dialogue II*, ed. Jack M. Tuell and Roger W. Fjeld (Minneapolis: Augsburg, 1991), 52-69; Thomas Edward Frank, *Polity, Practice and the Mission of The United Methodist Church*, updated edition (Nashville: Abingdon Press, 2002), 229-53; Roy Hunter Short, *Chosen to Be Consecrated: The Bishops of The Methodist Church, 1784–1968* (Lake Junaluska: Commission on Archives and History for the Council of Bishops, 1976); and Norman Woods Spellmann, *The General Superintendency in American Methodism, 1784–1870*, Ph.D. Dissertation, Yale University, April 1961.

16. For discussion of this development, see Frank, "Common Discipline" and Richey, "Twins" in *QTCC*. See also Thomas Edward Frank, *Polity, Practice, and the Mission of The United Methodist Church*, updated edition (Nashville: Abingdon Press, 2002) and Richey, *Conference*.

17. Lawrence, "Ordained Ministry," *QTCC*, 300-01.

18. Bishop Joseph E. Pennel Jr. was heard to make such a statement.

19. González, "Hispanic United Methodists," *PCM*, 241-53 and Shopshire, "Black Methodist Protestant," *PCM*, 193-216.

20. Richey, "Extension Ministries," *QTCC*.

21. See Chang, "Wages," *PCM*, 151-70; Troxell and Farris, "One Eye," *PCM*, 261-65; and Lawrence and Froehlich, "Clergy Compensation," *QTCC*, 287-300.

22. Memming, "Ministry," *PCM*, 129-48.

23. For continued episcopal commitment to itinerancy, see Judith Smith, "Bishops," *QTCC*, 209-10.

24. See John H. Wigger, *Taking Heaven by Storm: Methodism and the Rise of Popular Christianity in America* (New York and Oxford: Oxford University Press, 1998), 181-94.

25. See Donald E. Messer, ed. *Send Me?: The Itineracy in Crisis* (Nashville: Abingdon Press, 1991).

26. Richey, "Extension Ministries," *QTCC*, 175-85;

27. For amplification, see Richey, *Conference*, 63-94, 133-55.

28. This discussion depends on Richey, *Conference*, 155-58.

29. See David Lowes Watson, "Class Meetings" *DD* and his several books, *Accountable Discipleship: Handbook for Covenant Discipleship Groups in the Congregation* (Nashville: Discipleship Resources, 1985, 1984); *Class Leaders: Recovering a Tradition* (Nashville: Discipleship Resources, 1991); *Covenant Discipleship: Christian Formation through Mutual Accountability* (Nashville: Discipleship Resources, 1991); *The Early Methodist Class Meeting: Its Origins and Significance* (Nashville: Discipleship Resources, 1985); *Forming Christian Disciples: The Role of Covenant Discipleship and Class Leaders in the Congregation* (Nashville: Discipleship Resources, 1991).

3. Disciplined, Disciplining

1. *Works*, 7:659-60, # 475.

2. PRESS RELEASE: Presented by Melvin G. Talbert, Resident Bishop. Office of the Bishop, San Francisco Area The United Methodist Church at United Methodist Center West Sacramento, California, March 23, 1999—12:00 noon. Source: http://www.umc.org/umns/99/mar/157.htm Produced by United Methodist News Service. March 23, 1999 {157}. Used with permission of Bishop Talbert and UMNS.

3. See Thomas Edward Frank "Common Discipline," *QTCC* and *Polity, Practice, and the Mission of The United Methodist Church* (Nashville: Abingdon Press, 1997), especially 43-47, 99-102.

4. The letter dated BRISTOL, Sept. 10, 1784, and addressed "To Dr. COKE, Mr. ASBURY, and our Brethren in *NORTH-AMERICA*" can be seen in various places, among them, *Letters* (Telford), 7:237-38 and *Methodist Experience in America: A Sourcebook* (Nashville: Abingdon Press, 2000), 71-72.

5. (Philadelphia: Charles Cist, 1785).

6. 3rd ed., revised and enlarged (Nashville: Publishing House of the Methodist Episcopal Church, South, 1908), 532-602.

7. See the discussion in Behney/Eller, *History*, 76-79, 100-8.

8. Cartwright, "Discipline" *DD*.

9. See Sweet, *Methodists*, 552-679.

10. Perhaps most accessible in Tigert, *History*. See specifically Questions 27, 62, and 63, pp. 549 and 574. The former read "To Whom is the *Superintendent* amenable for his Conduct."

11. See Watson, "Class Meetings," *DD*.

12. Watson, "Class Meetings," *DD* and his *Accountable Discipleship: Handbook for Covenant Discipleship Groups in the Congregation* (Nashville: Discipleship Resources, 1985, 1984); *Class Leaders: Recovering a Tradition* (Nashville: Discipleship Resources, 1991); *Covenant Discipleship: Christian Formation through Mutual Accountability* (Nashville: Discipleship Resources, 1991); *The Early Methodist Class Meeting: Its Origins and Significance* (Nashville: Discipleship Resources, 1985); *Forming Christian*

Disciples: The Role of Covenant Discipleship and Class Leaders in the Congregation (Nashville: Discipleship Resources, 1991).

13. *Minutes of Several Conversations Between the Rev, Thomas Coke, LL. D., the Rev. Francis Asbury and Others, at a Conference, Begun in Baltimore, in the State of Maryland, on Monday, the 27th of December, in the Year 1784* (Philadelphia: Charles Cist, 1785), 15-17. Tigert, *History*, 554-56.

14. Cartwright, "Discipline," *DD*.

15. See in the current *Book of Discipline of The United Methodist Church* (1) under "Our Doctrinal Heritage" the sections entitled "Doctrine and Discipline in the Christian Life" and "General Rules and Social Principles" and (2) under "Our Doctrinal Standards and General Rules" the section entitled "The General Rules of The Methodist Church."

16. Cartwright, "Discipline," Schneider, "Connectionalism," Tucker, "Family and Midweek Worship," and Strong, "Middle and . . . Margins," *DD*.

17. Kreutziger, "Social Holiness," *CEMI*, 137-75, and "Lay Leadership," *QTCC*, 119-31.

18. Wesley, *Works*, 9, 69-79.

19. Wesley, *Works*, 9, 70-73.

20. In the section "Our Doctrinal Heritage," subsection "Doctrine and Discipline in the Christian Life," *Discipline*/UMC 1996, 46.

21. The lines dividing these several meanings and also those to be discussed are indeed fine. The third and fourth meanings are indeed close. We might distinguish them by noting that the third accents the human will and a life of obedience and the fourth accents the affections and the full range of expressions of life in the spirit.

22. See the chapter on "Itinerant," and Heitzenrater, "Connectionalism and Itinerancy," *CEMI*; Lawrence, "Ordained Ministry," *QTCC*; Campbell, *The Yoke of Obedience: The Meaning of Ordination in Methodism* (Nashville: Abingdon Press, 1988); and Lawrence and Froehlich, "Clergy Compensation," *QTCC*.

23. For a different way of making the case, one that reflects on the Christian understanding of marriage, see Bell, "Homosexuality," *QTCC*, 271-79.

24. McClain, "African American Methodists," *CEMI*; Gravely, "African-American . . . Memory," *PCM*; Shopshire, "Black . . . Methodist Protestant," *PCM*; Cartwright, "Discipline," *DD*; Schneider, "Connectionalism," *DD*; Strong, "Middle and . . . Margins," *DD*; Rowe, "Caucuses," *QTCC*; Kreutziger, "Social Holiness," *CEMI*.

25. Cartwright, "Discipline," *DD*, 99-127.

26. *Discipline*/UMC 1996, 65. The Articles of Religion of The Methodist Church contained the first affirmation, the classical Reformation or Lutheran formulation, but not the second that derives from the Calvinist or Reformed tradition (57).

27. Nolan B. Harmon, *The Rites and Ritual of Episcopal Methodism* (Nashville: Publishing House of the Methodist Episcopal Church, South, 1926), 356-57.

28. *Discipline*/ME 1940, 658. *Discipline*/UMC, *Book of Worship*/UMC 1964, 50. The contrast between the historic "discipline of Christ" and the recent "discipline of the Church" might tempt one to impious observations.

29. *Discipline*/UMC 1992, 232; *Book of Worship*, UMC, 1996, 670.

30. *Discipline*/UMC 1996, 170, 110-12.

31. *Discipline*/UMC 1996, 247, 248.

32. Smith, "Bishops," *QTCC*, 194-215.

33. *Calvin: Institutes of the Christian Religion*, ed. John T. McNeill; trans. and index

by Ford Lewis Battles, The Library of Christian Classics, 2 vols. (Philadelphia: The Westminster Press, 1960), II, 1229-30.

34. See Frank, *Polity*, 127-41.

35. John Tigert put it: "Since 1744 the two constant factors of Methodist polity, (1) a superintending and appointing power, and (2) a consulting body called the Conference, have been continuously operative. These two factors are constitutional or elemental in the government of Methodism." Tigert, *History*, 15.

36. Frank, "Common Discipline," *QTCC*, 219-31.

37. *Letters* (Telford), 7:37. To Samuel Bradburn, Oct. 28, 1780.

38. *Letters* (Telford), 7:101. To John Valton, Jan. 18, 1782.

39. *The Book of Discipline of The United Methodist Church*, 2000.

40. Frank, "Common Discipline," *QTCC*, 219-31.

41. *Letters* (Telford), 7:362. To Adam Clarke, Jan. 3, 1787.

42. *Works*, 3:511-12.

43. *Works*, 3:598.

44. See Carroll, "Small Congregations," *QTCC*, 140-50, especially 145-50, on the self-discipline on the part of the pastor requisite for effective leadership, even in the small congregation.

45. See *Who Will Go for Us?: An Invitation to Ordained Ministry* (Nashville: Abingdon Press, 1994) and *The Yoke of Obedience: The Meaning of Ordination in Methodism* (Nashville: Abingdon Press, 1988).

46. William H. Willimon, *Pastor: The Theology and Practice of Ordained Ministry* (Nashville: Abingdon Press, 2002). See especially chapters 11–13, but the concern runs through the book. See also his *Calling and Character: Virtues of the Ordained Life* (Nashville: Abingdon Press, 2000), chapter 2, where ethics is treated under the rubric of "character."

47. Thomas C. Oden, *Pastoral Theology: Essentials of Ministry* (San Francisco: Harper & Row, Publishers, 1983), 206. The first citation is his chapter title for pp. 206-19.

48. Ibid., 207.

49. Ibid., 209.

50. See, for instance, Robin W. Lovin, *Christian Ethics: An Essential Guide* (Nashville: Abingdon Press, 2000).

51. See "Discipline" in *The Interpreter's Dictionary of the Bible*, George Arthur Buttrick et al., eds., 4 vols. (New York and Nashville: Abingdon Press, 1962), 1:846, and "Discipline, Divine" in *The Interpreter's Dictionary of the Bible: Supplementary Volume*, Keith Crim et al., eds. (Nashville: Abingdon Press, 1976), 234-36.

4. Catholic

1. *Hymns*, Works, 7:97-98, #15.

2. The claim is Albert Outler's, made in "An Introductory Comment," to "Catholic Spirit," Works, 2:80. For bibliography, see Kenneth E. Rowe, comp. and ed., *United Methodist Studies: Basic Bibliographies*, 4th edition (Nashville: Abingdon Press, 1998) and Paul F. Blankenship, "Ecumenicity and the United Methodist Church," *EWM*, I, 743-45 and the various cross-references therein.

3. John Wesley, "Catholic Spirit," *Works*, 2:90-92.

4. Christian Newcomer, *The Life and Journal of the Rev'd Christian Newcomer, Late Bishop of the Church of the United Brethren in Christ. Written by Himself,* Transcribed, corrected, and translated by John Hildt (Hagerstown, Md.: F.G.W. Kapp, 1834), 216-27. Excerpts.

5. For further development of points in this paragraph, see Richey, "Family Meal, Holy Communion, and Love Feast: Three Ecumenical Metaphors," in Richey, ed., *Ecumenical and Interreligious Perspectives: Globalization in Theological Education* (Nashville: QR Books, 1992), 17-30.

6. "The United Brethren Record Early Annual and General Conferences," *MEA,* II, 1800b, 137-45.

7. See Richey, *Conference.*

8. "The Evangelical Association Records Early Annual and General Conferences," *MEA,* II, 1807, 152-55.

9. See Colin W. Williams, *John Wesley's Theology Today* (New York and Nashville: Abingdon Press, 1960), 13-22.

10. John Deschner, "United Methodism's Basic Ecumenical Policy," in Richey, ed., *Ecumenical and Interreligious Perspectives: Globalization in Theological Education* (Nashville: Quarterly Review Books, 1992), 45-57; and in *Perspectives,* 448-59.

11. *The Book of Discipline of The United Methodist Church,* 1996 or 2000, Part I. Those versions are referenced in the following unless otherwise noted.

12. The 2000 *Discipline* thus relocated to fore in "The Ministry of all Christians," the early paragraphs that in the 1996 *Discipline* had framed "Chapter One: The Local Church" and had logically defined the mission of the local church. Now the lead statement on the mission of the church as a whole and the ministry of all Christians is that previously given precisely for the local church. This represents a further step in what I have several places commented upon as the congregationalizing of Methodism. See especially Richey, "Twins," *QTCC,* 232-41.

13. For a different schematization see Love, "World Church," *QTCC,* 258-70.

14. *Discipline*/UMC 1996, ¶ 66B, 92.

15. For protocols adopted by General Conference, see *The Book of Resolutions of The United Methodist Church, 1996*: "The Church's Response to Ethnic and Religious Conflict," adopted 1996, 210-11; "Building New Bridges in Hope," on Jewish-Christian relations, adopted 1996, 189-97; "Prejudice Against Muslims and Arabs in the U.S.A.," adopted 1988, 352-53; "A Charter for Racial Justice Policies in an Interdependent Global Community," adopted 1980, 202-4, *and especially,* "Guidelines for Interreligious Relationships: 'Called to Be Neighbors and Witnesses,'" adopted 1980, 258-68.

16. On these dialogues, their status and the agreements issuing therefrom, see Geoffrey Wainwright, *Methodists in Dialog* (Nashville: Kingswood Books/Abingdon Press, 1995).

17. O'Malley, "Distinctive Witness," *DD,* 53-76.

18. Jones, "Methodist Theology," *DD,* 77-95; Langford, "Theology," *QTCC,* 45-50; Sano, "Contextual," *QTCC,* 51-61.

19. *Christian History* 65 (February 2000): 36-37. *CR* devotes the issue to the listing and places Mott alongside Billy Graham, William Seymour, Mother Teresa, Karl Barth, C. S. Lewis, John XXIII, Alexander Solzhenitsyn, John Paul II, and Martin Luther King Jr.

20. "Proposal for the Adoption of Church in Covenant Communion," 360-62, *The Book of Resolutions of The United Methodist Church, 1996.* Compare also in the 1996

Resolutions, "Act of Covenanting Between Other Christian Churches and the United Methodist Church," adopted 1992, 151-55; "COCU Consensus: In Quest of a Church of Christ Uniting," adopted 1988, 211-12; "Continuing Membership in the Consultation on Church Union," adopted 1992, 220-21; "Mutual Recognition of Members," adopted 1984, 324-26; "Support the Consultation on Church Union Proposal," adopted 1992, 413; "Toward an Ecumenical Future," adopted 1992, 415-16.

21. Campbell, "Future," *QTCC*, 9-23; Marler and Hadaway, "'Self-Authoring' Religious Identity," *CEMI*, 289-316; Guth and Green, "Statistical Portrait," *PCM*, 27-52; Carroll and Roof, "Congregations," *PCM*, 55-83; Olson and McKinney, "Leaders," *PCM*, 109-26. The literature on civil or public religion is immense. Numbered among such is my first book, co-edited with Donald G. Jones, *American Civil Religion* (New York: Harper & Row, 1974; San Francisco: Mellen Research University Press, 1990).

22. This was the North American rendition of Wesley's "To reform the Nation, particularly the Church, and to spread scriptural holiness over the land," as can be seen by comparing the first *Discipline* with the "Large Minutes," in Tigert, *History*, 535.

23. See Longfield, "Methodist Identities," *CEMI*, 95-113; Rowe, "Redesigning Churches," *CEMI*, 117-34; Schneider, "Connectionalism," *DD*, 131-57; Wright, "Public Education," *DD*, 179-95.

24. See Longfield, "Methodist Identities," *CEMI*, 95-113; Wright, "Public Education," *DD*, 179-95.

25. *Discipline*/UMC 1996, ¶ 64-70, pp. 84-106. See Donald K. Gorrell, "The Social Creed and Methodism Through Eighty Years," *Perspectives*, 386-99.

26. Love, "World Church," *QTCC*, 260-61, distinguished five types of global vision—global confessional, global interconfessional, extended-national confessional, regional confessional and regional interconfessional. See entries in *EWM*, II, 2600-02.

27. For the processes, within North America, that yielded Methodist varieties, see Richey, "Division," *QTCC*, 105-16; Cartwright, "Discipline," *DD*, 99-127; Schneider, "Connectionalism," *DD*, 131-57; Strong, "Middle and Margins," *DD*, 233-41.

28. Robbins, "Connection," *DD*, 197-212.

29. For chapters in the longer relation of black and white Methodists, see McClain, "African American Methodists," *CEMI*, 77-91; Gravely, "African-American in Memory," *PCM*, 175-90; Shopshire, "Black Methodist Protestant," *PCM*, 193-216; Cartwright, "Discipline," *DD*, 97-127; Richey, "Division," *QTCC*, 105-16; Sledge, "Mergers," *CEMI*, 205-18.

30. For perspective on and critique of the understanding of globalism implicit in the CPT proposals see Love, "World Church," *QTCC*, 258-70 and Robbins, "Connection," *DD*, 197-212.

31. On the strains and divisions within United Methodism, see Becker, "Local Mission," *CEMI*, 267-85; Marler and Hadaway, "'Self-Authoring' Religious Identity," *CEMI*, 289-316; Guth and Green, "Statistical Portrait," *PCM*, 27-52; Carroll and Roof, "Congregations," *PCM*, 55-83; Olson and McKinney, "Leaders," *PCM*, 109-26; Troxell and Farris, "One Eye," *PCM*, 257-73; Mathews, "Testimony, Voice," *PCM*, 279-304; Richey, "Division," *QTCC*, 105-16; Rowe, "Caucuses," *QTCC*, 242-57; Bell, "Homosexuality," *QTCC*, 271-79.

32. See Robert Wuthnow, *The Restructuring of American Religion* (Princeton: Princeton University Press, 1988) and *The Struggle for America's Soul* (Grand Rapids: William B. Eerdmans, 1989).

33. Early commentators employing "liberal and evangelical" as scholarly rubrics included Richard J. Coleman, *Issues of Theological Conflict: Evangelicals and Liberals* (Grand Rapids: William B. Eerdmans, 1972); James Davison Hunter, *American Evangelicalism: Conservative Religion and the Quandary of Modernity* (New Brunswick: Rutgers University Press, 1983); Richard Quebedeaux, *The Worldly Evangelicals* (San Francisco: Harper & Row, 1978); and R. Stephen Warner, *New Wine in Old Wineskins: Evangelicals and Liberals in a Small-Town Church* (Berkeley: University of California Press, 1988).

34. The contrast that James Davison Hunter employs in *Culture Wars* (New York: Basic Books, 1991) is "progressive and orthodox."

The "public and private" formulation of the two-party division for twentieth-century Protestantism derives from Jean Miller Schmidt, an argument accessible now in the published version of her dissertation, *Souls or the Social Order: The Two-Party System in American Protestantism* (Brooklyn: Carlson, 1991), and by Martin E. Marty in *Righteous Empire* (New York: The Dial Press, 1970). See also Dean R. Hoge, *Division in the Protestant House* (Philadelphia: Westminster Press, 1976).

A contrast of this worldly and otherworldly is drawn by David A. Roozen, William McKinney, and Jackson W. Carroll in *Varieties of Religious Presence* (New York: Pilgrim Press, 1984). Richard J. Mouw, "New Alignments: Hartford and the Future of Evangelicalism," in Peter L. Berger and Richard John Neuhaus, eds., *Against the World for the World* (New York: Seabury Press, 1976), contrasts the two parties as "ecumenical and evangelical."

35. "The Conversations Continue," GCCUIC Newsletter, Dec. 5, 1999, Web site, http://www.gccuic-umc.org/.

36. See on the various groupings within Methodism and the variety of concerns that unite them Rowe, "Caucuses," *QTCC*, 242-57; González, "Hispanic United Methodists," *PCM*, 241-53; Gravely, "African-American in Memory," *PCM*, 175-90; Bell, "Homosexuality," *QTCC*, 271-79; Kim, "Missions to Korea," *PCM*, 219-38; McClain, "African American Methodists," *CEMI*, 77-91; Richey, "Division," *QTCC*, 105-16; Sledge, "Mergers," *CEMI*, 205-18; Troxell and Farris, "One Eye," *PCM*, 257-73; Sano, "Contextual," *QTCC*, 51-61; Monk, "Campus Ministry," *CEMI*, 179-202.

37. For the evangelical account of this version of catholicity, see Riley B. Case, *Evangelical and Methodist: A Popular History* (Nashville: Abingdon Press, 2004) and James V. Heidinger II and Steve Beard, eds., *Streams of Renewal: Welcoming New Life into United Methodism* (Wilmore: Living Streams Publications, 2004). For the progressive account, see Leon Howell, *United Methodism @ Risk: A Wake-up Call*, study guide by Bishop C. Dale White and the Rev. Scott Campbell (Kingston, N.Y.: Information Project for United Methodists, 2003). The conspiratorial cabal of conservatism that this latter work discovers may, as evangelicals have protested, been overstated, but the general lines of affinity probably hold as the first essay in *Streams* indicates.

Postscript

1. *Works*, 9:41.

2. For an imperative to view those together, at least in thinking with Wesley, see Heitzenrater, "Connectionalism and Itinerancy," *CEMI*, 23-38.